THE INNOVATION MINDSET

THE

A Proven Method to Fuel

INNOVATION

Performance and Results

MINDSET

JENNIFER KENNY

Cataloguing in publication information is
available from Library and Archives Canada.

ISBN 978-1-77458-268-8 (paperback)
ISBN 978-1-77458-269-5 (ebook)
ISBN 978-1-77458-350-0 (audiobook)

Page Two
pagetwo.com

Edited by James Harbeck
Copyedited by Crissy Calhoun
Cover design and interior illustrations by Jennifer Lum
Interior design by Cameron McKague

jenniferkenny.com

*I would like to dedicate this book to
my daughter Julia who has been instrumental
in making this book happen. Thank you.*

Contents

Author's Note

WROTE THIS book for the innovators and explorers out there who seek to make the world a better place for all of us. Some of you, I've had the pleasure of working with. Many of you, I look forward to working with in the future.

Over the course of my career in research and innovation, I've discovered that corporate scientists, engineers, researchers, and innovators struggle deeply with the balance between investigative research and product development. Their best work fits somewhere between these two. I've worked at several research institutes, and over the years, I have observed that leadership also struggles to maintain this balance. How can we create the ideal structures to deliver new capabilities to your parent company, to the market, and to a broader audience? How do you do that while cultivating the research capacity of the people on your team? How do you do that while allowing for high degrees of emergence and exploration, which are essential for both incremental and disruptive innovation? How do you do this inside corporations where this is not yet the norm?

If these are questions you live with every day, then I wrote this book for you.

As a scientist and an engineer myself, I always balked at the idea that the dominant command-and-control approach to leadership and management was most effective, even though it seemed like the only option for leading and managing a team of researchers, innovators, engineers, and scientists. I always felt there had to be another and more effective way.

In my late twenties, I came across an elegant body of thought that allowed me to begin to answer these questions for myself. My first encounter was with the work of Terry Winograd and Fernando Flores, whom I had the honor of working with. Their book *Understanding Computers and Cognition: A New Paradigm for Design* remains game-changing. That book led me on a path of exploring design thinking and systems thinking; I also looked more deeply into self-organizing systems, self-organizing teams, how knowledge emerges, and how knowledge is both amplified and transferred. This was the root: it was where I started to ask myself, "How can I help others cultivate, structure, and design environments where people can be at their most creative and most innovative, while at the same time balancing the need to deliver measurable value, all within a committed time frame? In short, what can I teach that will help us innovate better together?"

I now believe, after many years of inquiry in this area, that practices are key to this. Our ability to consciously onboard new practices, to design new practices, to observe the practices of others, and to deconstruct, reconstruct, and embody those practices is absolutely pivotal for maintaining and growing our autonomy, our mastery, and our purpose.

In this book, I explore how to use practices to cultivate

these capabilities, as part of your own leadership and for and within your own teams. My goals are to introduce you to the power of practices and to show you how certain specific practices contribute towards your innovation capacity, enabling you to fuel performance and results in your research, in your innovation, and within your company.

I'm delighted you are reading this book, and I hope you get a lot out of it. If you do, in the spirit of serving others, please pass it on.

In gratitude,
Jennifer

1

Two Eyes, Two Ears, One Mouth

or, Common Sense about Work and Innovation

---

*"Human beings are born into a world of
conversations already going on."*

FERNANDO FLORES,
Conversations for Action and Collected Essays

THINK ABOUT innovation. Do you picture a light bulb going off above some genius's head? A lot of us do. And we think of Thomas Edison, the first genius to think of a light bulb: a solitary inventor, working thousands of hours in his lab to create something that transformed how we all live. It's the most common understanding of innovation: the Invention Model. It's a nice, clear image. And it's wrong.

If things were ever that simple, they certainly aren't now. As our world becomes more complex, our social ecosystems evolve and become more sophisticated, while innovation becomes progressively more complex. Innovation doesn't involve one person working alone. It involves people, and lots of them.

Innovation capacity is both a personal and a team capacity. Our personal likelihood of creating a moonshot innovation as an individual scientist or researcher shrinks as the complexity of our world increases. But our opportunities to create interdisciplinary or transdisciplinary innovation expand. (To quote Klaus Mainzer, "In recent time, innovations emerge from problem-oriented research overcoming traditional boundaries of disciplines (e.g., material research, energy, environment, health, aging society). If problem-oriented research is beyond former divisions of faculties, it is sometimes called 'transdisciplinary.' Interdisciplinary dialogues are needed to find transdisciplinary problems and new portfolios of technologies.")

Building our innovation capacity as individuals, teams, and organizations therefore requires that we become masterful at leading not only research but also the capacity development required for complex innovation. Sometimes this means crafting better practices.

The Three Levels of Innovation Capacity diagram shows the ladder we need to climb to reach our Innovation Capacity Maturity. We move from a pure product focus (think light bulbs) towards a human innovation focus, which requires a deep and broad understanding of the ecosystem within which we are innovating. As we proceed up the maturity ladder, we shift our understanding of innovation from ideas that deliver products to ideas that offer value, can come in many different forms, and result in the adoption of new practices within a community. If our goal is to become what I refer to as Innovation Superstars, our route involves developing our own and others' innovation capacities by cultivating advanced practices and an innovation mindset. It involves using our two eyes, two ears, and one mouth in ways we hadn't considered before.

The key is Human Innovation: a framework and approach for mobilizing people and transforming organizations to increase overall innovation capacity. The Human Innovation framework is designed to:

- Establish and support an innovation mindset

- Remove friction and support the innate drive of innovators

- Create an environment that supports autonomy while enabling efficiency

- Align practices with the existing environment to produce innovation

- Establish listening across any ecosystem to enable feedback and build mastery

Without attention to Human Innovation, we tend not to view innovation as a team practice or a learned capability that needs to be intentionally built up within a team over time. We're still looking for light bulb moments: we believe that we can hire a genius innovator, and then magic will happen. But if we have only one bulb, that bulb ultimately burns out. When we follow the Invention Model, we struggle to produce sustainable innovation. Human Innovation is the missing link for both enhancing our individual and team innovation capacities and for creating successful practices for communities. This book shows you how to use Human Innovation to drive innovation in your work, at your company, and beyond.

The Practice/Impact Model

I want to show you another model to understand how the power of practices can support the development of our innovation capacity. The Practice/Impact Model (see page 12) shows the increases in sophistication and impact as we move up the ladder from basic individual abilities to innovating with teams.

On the operational level, we begin with organic talents (x) and increase in sophistication to skills (2x) and competencies (4x). From there, we level up into the generative, starting with individual deliberate practices (20x). At that point, the increase in sophistication becomes collective, and we see richer conversations (60x), better design (70x), and ultimately agile co-inventive processes (100x).

The Three Levels of Innovation Capacity

	Maturity	You Have/Are	You Are	Innovation Capacity
Product Innovation + Human Innovation + Ecosystem Innovation				
3	Innovation Superstars	• Global game changers • Attracting top talent • Amplifying the ecosystem	• A game changer	• 90 percent
Product Innovation + Human Innovation				
2	Robust Innovation Process	• Committed partnerships across the ecosystem • A compelling, sophisticated global vision	• A thought leader	• 70 percent
	Functional Innovation Process	• Co-invention practices • Growing value chain understanding • Burgeoning ecosystem awareness	• Leading • Beginning to have fun	• 60 percent

The Three Levels of Innovation Capacity

	Maturity	You Have/Are	You Are	Innovation Capacity
Product Innovation				
1	**Beginning Innovation**	• A product road map • Feature/ capability teams • An agreed critical path	• Optimistic	• 30 percent
	Unstable	• Demo death marches • Technical debt • An unclear plan or critical path	• Burned out	• 20 percent
	Silos	• Silos working on cool stuff • Untested ideas	• Maxed out	• 20 percent
	Individuals	• A motley crew of smart individuals	• Herding cats	• 10 percent

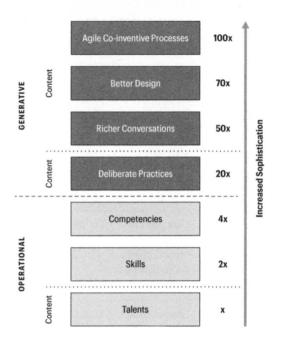

The Practice/Impact Model

Operational Capacity

On the operational level, our talents are what we innately have. Our skills are things we choose to teach ourselves and learn from others. Our competencies are the things we regularly focus on, and we use a combination of knowledge, ability, and skill to develop competencies over time. Think of it like playing doubles tennis: if your partner is naturally talented, you will probably win a few games, but if your partner has also built skills on top of their talent and honed them into competencies by regularly practicing for continuous improvement, then you'll win a lot more—especially if you're keeping up with your partner. These areas of focus are what I refer to as the Operational Human Capacities.

Operational Human Capacity is in part what organizations harness when they hire people for their skills and competencies. But what is required for innovation is beyond what a firm might receive when someone walks in the door: it's generated when you align individuals' existing capacities with structural practices designed to facilitate innovation.

Generative Capacity

The foundation of Generative Capacity is generative practices, which originate with an individual seeking to ignite in others their abilities to create or produce what is important to them. Generative behaviors support our own growth by supporting the growth of others, helping them progress towards their own autonomy, mastery, and purpose.

Thomas Edison liked to say that genius was 1 percent inspiration and 99 percent perspiration. But we can fall into the trap of thinking that all that perspiration is individual. The truth is that most of it is in the top half of the Practice/Impact Model. As Peter Denning and Robert Dunham point out, 90 percent of the effort in successful innovation is in getting communities to adopt it. No matter how earth-shattering our research and our inventions are, unless we can show how they might be adopted in a community and how we might learn from that adoption process, we are inventors but not innovators. To innovate, you need to co-invent. You need to work with other people. You need to ask questions—and listen to the answers.

Over time, individuals who develop their own practices either become role models for others or directly help others design practices that increase their innovative capacity. But the first step is understanding the power of deliberately creating and adopting practices. If we are not deliberate, we can fall into the trap of building practices on broken ideas about how things should be done. For example, we might create great inventions and try to lob them over the wall to product development, expecting a miracle. But when we focus on creating and adopting effective practices, we seek out new distinctions and build interpretations that push and stretch the common assumptions of "how things should be done" or "how things are done around here." We can build fresh practices around our new distinctions and interpretations, which amplify both our own impact and the impact of these practices. This leads us to richer conversations, better design, and agile, co-inventive practices.

Six Steps and Three Engines

I am going to introduce two more diagrams to get us rolling. The Six Step Practice Model is loosely how this book is organized. As we follow it, we will climb the ladder of Human Innovation, from basic individual ability to agile co-inventive team practices. We will question common sense and see a new future for work. And we'll learn how to foster innovation by observing, experiencing, and amplifying—and how to scale it to innovate better with your team and in the broader ecosystem.

The essential first step in the development of any practice is to distinguish—to observe distinctions. Every discipline has its own distinctions and common language; those distinctions help us identify the actions, objects, artifacts, interpretations, technology, tools, and concepts that are relevant and valuable to those who practice the discipline and those who benefit from it. Regardless of the domain or discipline, there are key distinctions that we need to learn in order to contribute to and engage in it.

A simple example of a distinction is when a surgeon is in an operating theater, and she turns around to the attending

The Six Step Practice Model

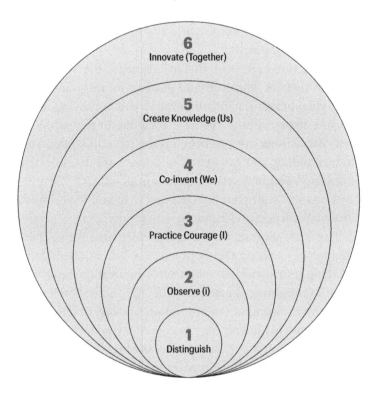

6
Innovate (Together)

5
Create Knowledge (Us)

4
Co-invent (We)

3
Practice Courage (I)

2
Observe (i)

1
Distinguish

nurse and says, "Scalpel." There are many kinds of scalpels, but the context in which the surgeon makes the request means the attending nurse knows which scalpel to give to her.

Sometimes these shared distinctions are built up over considerable time, and sometimes they are a requirement to be in the operating room in the first place. In this case, the word *scalpel* and the context (and probably also the presurgery preparation) distinguish for both the surgeon and the nurse exactly which scalpel is meant.

You can find examples of distinctions in pretty much every sport. Players use in-sport distinctions to effectively communicate with each other in what could be considered shorthand, but if you play close attention, it's distinctions. The rugby term *scrum* is now also a term that we use in Agile software development.

Distinctions are your shared language, the vocabulary used to discuss what you and your team are pointing to, observing, building standards around, and improving. What are you distinguishing? What is meaningful to you? What new distinctions can you bring to the table to stretch your understanding and help you build more robust, effective innovation and innovation leadership practices? What distinctions will shift your mindset and help you to co-invent, create knowledge, and innovate with others?

The other diagram I want to introduce here is the Three Engines of Capacity Development. As I mentioned above, building your own and your team's innovation capacities relies on the power of practices. Effective innovation leaders are themselves engines of innovation capacity development. Pay attention to not only how you develop your own practices but also how you use those practices of observing, experiencing, and amplifying to help your team build its observation capacity and how you set up immersive experiences to help them embody new practices and amplify each other. And then how you further scale that into the extended ecosystem.

Unlike the other diagrams, this one depicts not a ladder that you climb but a cycle that you constantly repeat. As you observe and embody your own practices and then help your team create knowledge and innovate better together, you will see that the practices that I introduce are recursive: the more you observe and embody them yourself, the more effective you are at helping your team to do the same for themselves—and vice versa.

Now let's get started.

The Three Engines of Capacity Development

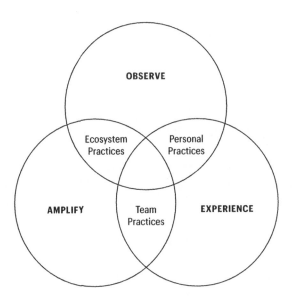

How to Understand Other People

Every human being on the planet relates to the world differently. Every human being has a different lived experience. I love the massive, rich diversity these differences offer us. This diversity is significant; it implies that we are all discrete pieces of the puzzle. Differences in experience and perspective allow us to be more perceptive and to better observe the entire picture. But any one of us will never be able to understand everything about how other people see the world. We can only see things through our own eyes, and some things that are obvious essential truths to one person are completely invisible to another.

We can, however, expand our experience of the world. We can broaden our insight by being deeply aware of our own perspective's limitations, or our cognitive blindness, by asking ourselves: Why do they say what they say? Do what they do? Focus on what they focus on? Why that particular passion? (Sometimes we can even ask them directly!) By practicing this, we can increase our chances of connecting and working with others successfully, enhance our enjoyment of the world, and expand our influence and impact in support of ourselves and others. When we have more lenses through which to consider the variable challenges we encounter, we broaden our mutual understanding. That offers us both a wider and a finer set of tools with which to relate to those around us.

Here are five steps you can take to put this in practice.

1. Admit That Adulting Is a Game

I love the millennial term *adulting*, because it makes it sound like what it truly is: a silly practice of pretending that we're in control and that we know, with some certainty, what is going on. This is obviously a pretense. We do, in fact, live in a world where adults are supposed to be all-knowing experts. While it is good to point out when we are pretending to know the rules and their function, acknowledging this absurdity clashes with our common sense. The overarching common sense at play in the world is that we all know what we're doing, and that we simply must.

2. Accept That Not Knowing Is Part of the Human Condition

You are not stupid and there is nothing wrong with you. You've been socialized to believe that you are supposed to be in control and know everything—or at the very least, as an adult, that you should know an awful lot about an awful lot. Knowledge acquisition gets prioritized, while growing in wisdom is sidelined. Wisdom is about mindset, perspective, interpretation, context, judgment, integrity, and applied learned experience. Wisdom requires the humble acknowledgment of your own limitations, and it demands that we see the landscape of what we do not (and could not possibly) know.

3. Give Yourself the Gift of the Mindset Shift

Begin by working to accept that you don't know what you don't know, that you can't see what you can't see! Not only is awareness of our own ignorance okay, but it is also humble and wise. Once we let go of pretending that we are all-knowing experts, we can genuinely invite others to offer us their interpretations of the world, of our vision, of our practices.

4. Know That We Are Better Together

No matter how great a genius you are (or think you are), you still have only one window on the world. There will always be someone who can offer a lens, ask a question, or pose a solution that you might never consider. A broad range of perspectives is almost inevitable in any organic human social setting. Acknowledging our numerous vantage points helps us to see the whole picture. It's how humans have survived and thrived as a species. We are social animals. In sharing our different interpretations of the world, we are collectively more intelligent than we could ever be individually. Knowledge is cumulative and collaborative.

5. Give Up Being in Control and Play the Wisdom Game!

Wisdom is a game. Games are fun things you do with other people. When we choose to switch tacks to play the wisdom game, we commit to expanding our understanding of what is possible in joyful interaction with other people. Relinquishing control is what makes room for unexpected possibilities. This helps us to see things that we could not have imagined. In co-invention and partnership with others, we can accomplish things that, on our own, we could not dream up. As other people offer additional viewpoints, our vision expands. Through the process of helping each other witness the wholeness and complexity of our world, we can learn better together and better innovate.

When I talk about sharing viewpoints, I am *not* talking about feedback. What we call *feedback* is generally clumsy, reflexive attempts at finding faults and weaknesses. And when it's unsolicited, it's likely to be destructive. Although it is important to solicit perspectives from our peers, and to try to understand their perspectives in good faith, seek permission before outlining the limitations of other people's perspectives. If you recognize your own biases (we all have them!), you could perhaps catch yourself in a default need to be right and instead commit to be in wonder. Say to yourself, "Oh, she is seeing something I'm not seeing. I wonder what that is?" This admission allows you to practice your wisdom and potentially expand your knowledge. The benefit is threefold: your relationship with this knowledgeable person is strengthened by your humility; you have actively practiced personal wisdom; and you have a more detailed understanding of the limitations of your own knowledge.

Common Sense and What It Means

The starting point for Human Innovation, the first inning in the wisdom game, is common sense: the unspoken frame of reference in which we operate, interpret the world, learn, and engage with each other. We need to observe common sense, question common sense, and stop taking common sense for granted. We need to speak the unspoken and see if it's actually true.

This is not easy. It's like asking a fish to describe what they're swimming in—or a person to analyze the air they're breathing. Have you ever stopped to notice and question what you and the people around you think and feel about the value of work, for instance? Probably not, yet we are impacted by it every day.

Why does observing common sense matter? Think about some things that were common sense twenty-five years ago. If you wanted to read, you got a book or magazine; if you had to pay for something, you used cash or a credit card; if you were going to an event, you carried a ticket; if you wanted to listen to music, you put on a CD or tape player or a radio; and if you wanted to talk to someone far away, you used a telephone. Common sense said different functions needed different things to perform them, and that anything that tried to do a whole bunch of different things wouldn't perform any of them as well. And now, twenty-five years later, we have smartphones that do all those things and more, and often do them better.

Although other technological advancements have also had sweeping impacts, the iPhone demonstrates the kind of innovation that shifts our common sense. The iPhone, nearly unthinkable twenty-five years ago, has become part of our background of obviousness. Consider the rapid spread of QR codes: the operational assumption is that any ordinary person can scan a digital barcode with the camera on their smartphone and get instant access to a website.

When you begin to consider common sense, your answers to the question "What is work?" may shift. After the pleasure of years spent working with some of the most brilliant minds in research, I have come to believe that our collective struggle to shift from invention to innovation comes from a very deep-rooted misunderstanding of what work is. I propose to you that our common-sense understanding of work is reducing our innovation capacity.

In 1986, Fernando Flores did some beautiful work with Terry Winograd in coauthoring *Understanding Computers and Cognition*, which they called—accurately in hindsight, but quite boldly at the time—"a new paradigm for design." Winograd and Flores claimed that we invent our future in language. Instead of the future being something that happens *to* us, they argue that we invent our future in how we make declarations, offers, and promises to each other.

What does this have to do with work? As the saying goes, the best way for us to predict the future is to create it. But how do you do that if, for example, you're the VP of a group tasked with bringing amazing new solutions, products, or services to market? How do you begin to think about helping your people innovate to the point where you are actually creating the future as opposed to being a laggard in the market? You start by speaking the unspoken to see if it's really true.

How Does Work Work?

Our current common-sense understanding of work comes from around 1913, when humans started automating factories. Factory owners like Henry Ford brought in people who had very little education, who had never worked in organized team manufacturing before. They'd worked in organized teams on farms very effectively, so they knew how to work together. But because of the nature of production lines in 1913 and the layout of the factory floor, work was broken down into its smallest subcomponents because people didn't have the education to be able to understand the full process of assembling, for example, a car. One person's work was a tiny piece of what needed to be done. And the next person did the next tiny piece, and the next person did the next tiny piece, and so on. That was incredibly effective for building our civilization's manufacturing prowess. If you drove or took a train to work, you benefited from production line manufacturing. But when you got to work, did it still benefit you there?

Our common-sense understanding of work came from the production line. It came from the idea that work is a series of small, oftentimes repetitive tasks that can be subdivided among a team of people. Today we're using robots to do a lot of this manufacturing work, but the concept is still the same: we are still breaking work into small component parts. We get certain inputs, which might be raw materials or information; we ask a human being to do some processing; we might ask a computer or a robot to do some processing; and we produce a certain output. Input, process, output—or I-P-O for short.

This is a linear process, with no feedback loops built in. It is predicated on a person doing a discrete piece of work with little attention paid to what's going on around them and requiring very little context. It was designed to have this level of simplicity because it was the most efficient way to exploit the capacity of the labor force available.

But work has become a lot more complex in the past forty to fifty years, particularly as technology and its effects have accelerated in the last twenty to twenty-five years. We now have two to three generations of people with increasing levels of education who are more adept around technology. But as individuals and on teams, we're not necessarily more sophisticated in how we engage and coordinate and co-invent with each other. This undermines our ability to innovate, our ability to leverage technology to innovate, and our ability to build innovation as a practice and capacity in our organizations. If we treat people as discrete entities working on tiny, focused pieces of work with minimal context, we're missing out on leveraging their intelligence and education.

As technologies have allowed us to be less formal and less structured about work, we have pushed for more collaboration and co-invention, and it's almost as if human beings have realized their capabilities as their education levels improved. But now the technology is struggling to keep up with us— because it was built on this input-process-output way of thinking about work.

Winograd and Flores offer a different way of thinking about work rather than the old common-sense way, where work is the completion of a set of tasks. They invite us to look at work as the coordination of action between customers and performers to produce customer satisfaction. With this interpretation, work moves away from the tasks that I need to do and into the realm of those I'm engaging with. Who is my customer, both internal and external? How am I going to design and co-invent with them? What is the most effective way for me to deliver my offer, my contribution, my support for what they're trying to accomplish? And for them to do the same for me?

By thinking of work in this way and asking ourselves these questions, we begin to contextualize the work we're doing and the value we're producing. The work that we do is not driven by technology, but the reverse: we're the ones who are initiating the work in the first place. Over time, we see that all work does not come from our email inboxes or task lists. All work is initiated by a human being somewhere in the process. We become more sophisticated in our interpretations and ability to negotiate when we understand who initiated the work and why that work matters to them. We do a lot less "work for the sake of work," or to look busy, and we fall down a lot fewer rabbit holes. We have context. We've moved from the input-process-output concept of work to it being the conversations people have between customers and performers to produce customer satisfaction.

How can we use this language-based understanding to distinguish what's going on at work, so that we can become smarter, more powerful observers of the workflow within our organization? Our current common sense is that language is a vehicle for human beings to communicate information to each other. That's the input-process-output way of thinking: I communicate information to you, and you gather information from me. It's very linear and limited: you become a receptacle for the information that I give to you, as opposed to us having a collaborative conversation that we engage in together.

If, on the other hand, work is a series of collaborative conversations, I need to take into account how it is you're going to listen to what I am saying, how you're going to interpret it, how you're going to deploy it, and how you're going to engage with me. We begin to think differently about language, about it as more than information flowing back and forth. As we'll discover in chapter 2, we start to invent the future in language. And when we stop to question common sense, we can invent a new world of work that turns everything around.

I believe innovation is a practice, so I have included Key Practices at the end of each chapter to enable you to put the innovation mindset into practice in your daily work.

Each exercise is set up for you to observe a new distinction, to practice it with your team or in your work in general, as well as recommendations for ways to incorporate this practice into your daily work. You will build your innovation mindset and supporting practices.

Key Practice: Observing Common Sense and Being in Wonder

How do you observe, question, and move beyond common sense, by yourself or with your team? Here's a practice you can institute.

1. Pick a Topic

You can pick any topic that you think might be causing you or your team to be stuck or to have recurring breakdowns. For example, "We spend a lot of time trying to prove our point to each other, we argue a lot..."

2. Look at What's "Obvious"

Ask questions to interrogate the common sense. What essential assumption is validating the topic? For example, "Common sense says it's good to be right."

3. Speculate On What Might Be More Effective

What might be a more effective common sense for your team? For example, "Is it better to be *right* or to be *effective*?"

Don't expect a simple answer. Remember: context matters. It's still important to get your math right, but when it comes to management, leadership, and strategy, *right* becomes an opinion, and it is almost always better to be effective.

4. Discuss This with Your Team

If we decided to commit to distinguish between conversations about mathematics and conversations about management, leadership, strategy, technology transfer, etc., and then to play the "better to be effective versus to be right" game, how might conversations go differently?

5. Practice

Once you do this at four to six meetings, people will get the hang of it and begin to use it as a practice for furthering the conversation with less friction. They'll gradually move towards co-invention and better, faster decision-making.

6. Build the Muscle of Observing Common Sense for Yourself

You don't have to limit yourself to interrogating the obvious in work contexts. If you really want to build this muscle, you can do it almost anywhere:

- Listening to the news

- Reading articles

- Listening to podcasts

- Listening to your kids (who, if they are under twenty years old, are having common sense drilled into them all day every day)

2

Innovation Demands Courage

or, How to Create Customers with the Magic of Language

"Life has no meaning. Each of us has meaning and we bring it to life. It is a waste to be asking the question when you are the answer."

JOSEPH CAMPBELL

THE 2015 Accenture U.S. Innovation Survey of three thousand workers across industries discovered that "while 48 percent of C-level respondents believe their workplaces encourage innovative thinking, only 30 percent of individual contributors agree." Meanwhile, 84 percent of executives considered their future success to be very or extremely dependent on whether innovative thinking is happening in their office. That's quite a gap.

If work is our dominant place of practice, where we spend most of our time thinking, putting effort into action, and carrying out challenges, then implementing innovative thinking inside our office life both allows us to exercise our creativity at work, which can be immensely satisfying, and offers our best and most flexible thinking to our workplace successes. But thinking is not enough. You may as well be sitting at your desk daydreaming unless you can do something with it—something involving other people, because, as we know already, that's where innovation happens.

I find it useful to distinguish between two kinds of innovation:

1 Incremental or iterative innovation

2 Discontinuous or game-changing innovation

They are both valuable and necessary, and they have a lot in common. Both require:

- Thinking and reflection

- A desire to improve things

- A commitment to serve others—whether it's one person or one million—and make their lives better or easier

- Deep listening to what matters to yourself and others

- The ability to step back from a situation to see the bigger patterns

- Tools, approaches, and frameworks for design

- A sophisticated understanding of what is considered valuable in the context

- A willingness to make offers, and maybe not be heard

- A first adopter

All of us are capable of innovative thinking, and therefore we all have a chance of creating both incremental and discontinuous innovation. However, that is like saying that we are all capable of playing cards and have a chance of getting a royal flush in poker. Moments that produce discontinuous innovation are rare. Circumstance has to align with preparedness, and there is the unquantifiable element of good luck. As Douglas Osheroff said, "Most advances require both insight and good fortune."

Louis Pasteur famously said, "Chance favors only the prepared mind." I hear people talking about being in the right place at the right time. However, that can take courage—the courage to stretch beyond our comfort zone and listen carefully in order to serve those in our immediate and extended network.

Courageous Discomfort

There's a popular story about the nineteenth-century Antarctic explorer Ernest Shackleton. The story goes that he took out a short advertisement in the London *Times*:

> MEN WANTED for hazardous journey, small wages, bitter cold, long months of complete darkness, constant danger, safe return doubtful, honor and recognition in case of success.

Although historians doubt whether Shackleton himself took out the advertisement, the narrative is an inspiring one: five thousand people applied! Ultimately twenty-eight men (one of whom was a stowaway, so compelling was the narrative) and sixty-nine dogs went on the expedition with Shackleton.

The modern workplace carries with it a much lower chance of icy death (although some of us may relate to "long months of complete darkness"), but Shackleton has a lot to teach us about living in a state of courageous discomfort. He pursued discontinuous innovation and also relied on iterative innovation. On the one hand, Shackleton was part of the Age of Antarctic Exploration—he was not the first to explore the Antarctic, and he learned from those before him. On the other hand, his journey was not attempted again until 1958, fifty-one years later; in this respect, he exemplifies discontinuous innovation. And he exemplified both types of innovation in his desire to explore the unexplored for the sake of humanity.

Courageous discomfort isn't about seeking discomfort for its own sake. It means being comfortable with being uncomfortable so we can learn. The Courageous Discomfort diagram maps this out: learning slows down when our personal narrative is "I know what is going on here, I am sure

I am right, and I can't not be right." We lose the ability to see things in a new light. If, however, we are curious and comfortable with discomfort, we position ourselves to live in wonder, in a constant state of inquiry.

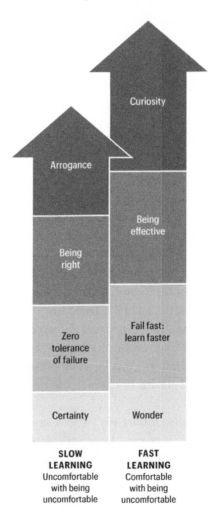

Courageous Discomfort

Curiosity

Arrogance

Being effective

Being right

Zero tolerance of failure

Fail fast: learn faster

Certainty

Wonder

SLOW LEARNING
Uncomfortable with being uncomfortable

FAST LEARNING
Comfortable with being uncomfortable

Our culture is one in which certainty and being right are elevated and lauded. We were taught to admire confident people who stand on their principles and never show the weakness of changing their minds or admitting they were wrong. It is very hard to be an innovative thinker in a culture like this. It takes quite a lot of courage to swim against that current. But what do you think it feels like to work in an environment where wonder prevails? Where we can fail fast and learn faster because there's no penalty for not being right the first time? Where we can focus on being effective, give rein to curiosity, and think for ourselves? It might feel like, "I am not sure what is going on here, but there may be cool opportunities for me, and I like that."

When I used to go to an art gallery, museum, or dance performance, I'd find myself immediately overwhelmed. Visual art in its immediacy carries a lot of emotional information. If the emotional realm is not your most natural realm—if, say, you're a facts and figures kind of person—this sort of high-frequency emotional environment can feel daunting and claustrophobic. You may assume that your feeling response to the art is somehow incorrect. The kind of "beginner's mind" that visual art asks us to engage can feel both disquieting and alien. The practice of sifting through a mixture of surfacing emotions demands from us bravery, honesty, and a relinquishment of knowingness. This is courageous discomfort. We have to be comfortable with ambiguity, uncertainty, our own beginner status, and a context in which there is often no right answer. It's easy and tempting to wave it away—but then we would never learn new things about ourselves.

Sometimes the biggest challenges are the ones we can pretend aren't there at all. You can stay at home, warm and safe. But meanwhile, people are signing up to join Ernest Shackleton.

Encouraging Innovative Thinking

If you believe, as I do, that everyone can be innovative and that this curious state encourages innovation, then each human has the capacity to reimagine the future to our collective advantage. We all have something to offer, a new perspective to bring and cultivate. A unique and different lived experience that grants us a different wisdom and perspective. Wonder is the most effective state for learning. To quote Ellen Parr, "The cure for boredom is curiosity. There is no cure for curiosity."

Being in wonder is like a baby learning to walk. Babies seem propelled by a desire to engage with the world around them. They discover that moving around on their own allows them to see more, experience more, explore better. Not knowing what they are likely to experience, or even how to name the objects they come into contact with, doesn't diminish their curious impulses. A desire for exploration pushes them forward. They fall down a thousand times and always get back up. They don't judge themselves or get frustrated by their inability to stand up straight; they simply keep trying. And they are discerning! They learn from every fall.

The human brain—the command center of the entire body—is not fully developed at birth. A newborn's brain is about a quarter of the size of the average adult brain. Incredibly, it doubles in size in the first year and keeps growing to about 80 percent of adult size by age three and 90 percent (nearly fully developed) by age five. We do our most accelerated brain development in our first five years, and the predisposition most commonly associated with small children is *wonder*. They also seem to have boundless energy.

Energy enables exploration, but wonder enables energy. Wonder is the genius ingredient that transforms effort into innovation. Sustaining this state requires the most humility. It is effectively our self-talk that says, "I'm not sure what is going on here, but there may be new opportunities, and I like that." Edison made more than a thousand variations on a light bulb before he found one that worked:

> Before I got through, I tested no fewer than six thousand vegetable growths and ransacked the world for the most suitable filament material.
>
> The electric light has caused me the greatest amount of study and has required the most elaborate experiments. I was never myself discouraged or inclined to be hopeless of success. I cannot say the same for all my associates. *Genius is one percent inspiration and ninety-nine percent perspiration.*

Ideally, when wonder meets ambition, we hear, "I believe there are opportunities in this situation, and I am committed to working hard to make them happen." It is an accelerant for learning that may require six thousand painstaking attempts, but it is still faster than anything else. Like a baby learning to walk, our desire to explore pushes us forward, whether we know what is immediately in front of us or not.

And when you're working with other people—innovating together rather than inventing by yourself in a workshop— wonder demands deep listening to what matters to yourself and others and the ability to step back from a situation to see the bigger patterns. Both are requirements for innovative thinking. If we are lucky and we make an effort to practice the routines of innovative thinking, on our best days, we are at the same time an overjoyed tottering baby, the intrepid Shackleton, and the endlessly persistent Edison. And together, we are inventing the future.

It Takes Courage to Invent the Future

It may seem odd to say that we invent the future, but there is growing evidence that our understanding of reality as something "out there" is not accurate. To quote popular physicist Carlo Rovelli, "The relationship between two objects is not something contained in one or the other of them: it is something more besides."

In an article in *MIT Technology Review*, Michael Reilly writes that while we have long believed that we directly experience reality, perceptions are continually shaped by our memories, expectations, and moods. They change what we see, hear, feel, and taste. This predictive coding helps us interpret all the messy sensory data our brains receive. It means we don't *experience* reality—we *interpret* it, and in doing so, we can navigate it. Coupled with our new understanding of the power of language, we can create different opportunities and possibilities for ourselves. We can *invent* our future.

This idea can be overwhelming. Without methods, practices, or processes, we can feel directionless, lacking a way to engage with such a significant shift in understanding.

Our future is an unknown quantity. I want us to have a hand in shaping how it plays out. The more we develop our skills and abilities to influence how the future plays out, the better for us! If we are invested in better outcomes for ourselves and those around us, we should begin to develop methods and practices for engaging courageously in this kind of invention. It is essential that we drive the invention of our own futures at work. It requires a sophisticated understanding of the situation and identifying, in context, what is considered valuable. You guessed it: more innovative thinking practices.

In my coaching practice, I was working with an HR manager—we'll call him Quincy. He was the business partner for a large technical team. He knew that he could more effectively support the team if he better understood their work. In conversation together, we identified that he is a very skilled listener. He was also exceptionally good at taking observant notes, surfacing outstanding issues, and pointing out areas that might lack resolution. I realized that a good next step for him, considering this skill set, was to chair senior-level team meetings. The combination of his skill set and his desire to improve the kind of effective support he could offer his team led us to think about positioning him in this role.

However, when I suggested this to Quincy, his immediate response was "I can't chair those meetings!" So I sat with him and we identified everything associated with chairing a meeting. After we had developed a realistic idea of what would be involved, and he got clear about how his existing skills aligned with it, he made the suggestion to the division head. The division head was absolutely delighted, because she wanted to engage and participate in the meetings herself. This courageous offer let my client simultaneously make himself more valuable to the division chair, learn a lot more about the business, and build trust with the rest of the executive team. He had invented his future.

Our Words Invent Our Future

In 1955, one of the era's leading philosophers, John L. Austin, presented a series of lectures called How to Do Things with Words. His idea was that in saying certain words, we are also taking action. For example, when someone standing at an altar during a wedding ceremony says "I do," they are not simply observing a fact, they are committing to a future: "I promise to participate in this relationship with you, and I promise to uphold the traditional norms of our community with respect to this marriage." When the leaders of a country make a formal declaration of war, they change the present condition and the future possibilities for hundreds of thousands, and sometimes millions, of people. Such moments of utterance are speech acts: acts of social creation.

Speech acts happen on smaller scales, too. A promise is a promise, and while the enforceable consequences for breaking a promise aren't the same for all promises—they range from mildly disappointing someone to being imprisoned—when we say "I promise to pay" or "I promise to show up for work," we are committing to a different future for ourselves and another person, team, or company. Promises, vows, and formal declarations aren't the only speech acts. Making an offer is also a speech act: it commits to a future, on the condition the offer is accepted. What's more, it doesn't wait for someone else to ask—it takes the lead. One of the most powerful ways to participate in the invention of your future is to take the lead. (As the old saying goes, if you're not the lead dog, the view never changes.) The most effective way to take the lead is to make an offer to someone else.

It sounds simple, but it's actually quite difficult. In the old idea of work, we're trained to wait until someone asks us to do something. Once you break out of this mindset and start making offers to those around you, you become the main character in your own story. These offers need to be carefully crafted, well-designed, and thoughtful offers, the result of active listening, but this kind of offering positions us as contributors of value within our companies. We position ourselves to innovate.

A former client of mine—I'll call her Astrid—was the senior director responsible for a small team. There were three other adjacent teams that she also had sufficient technical competence to be able to head up. Astrid's team and the three others all reported temporarily to a senior person—I'll call him Doug. Astrid suspected Doug was struggling to maintain the bandwidth to manage in combination with his many other responsibilities. You can see the offer Astrid could make: to take over all four teams. But there was a problem: Astrid had garnered a reputation for being overly ambitious. That caused friction in a team-oriented workplace. She didn't want to perpetuate that reputation, so she was afraid to make the offer. She needed to develop the courage to make an offer that might be rejected—and she also needed to work out how to make the offer in a way that would succeed.

Astrid and I sat down and drafted a speculative list of what Doug's concerns might be. Crafting this offer required thinking and reflection. Together, we tried to position her offer to demonstrate her commitment to serve others, as well as leverage her ability to step back from a situation to see the bigger patterns. She and I wrote out concerns Doug might have, so that she could say, "Here is how I would like to address your concerns. This is not about me getting promoted. This is not about me taking on more and more responsibility just to have more people reporting to me. This is about me making an offer to support both you and the company as a whole."

Astrid built and presented the offer to Doug. He made some small changes, but overall he liked it. With his support, Astrid went to the CEO and executive team and made the offer. What they saw was a senior director, Astrid, stepping up and taking on a small division, which freed a very senior-level person, Doug, to advise rather than do operational management. The CEO and the executive team were delighted, because they gained more bench strength with somebody stepping up and taking on more responsibility. Of course, they accepted the offer.

When you have not already been declared the leader, the most effective way to take the lead is to make an offer. It sounds simple but is difficult to do because hierarchical command-and-control prevails in most environments. In this way of working and organizing, we are trained to do what we're told and wait until someone asks us to act. Sometimes we're waiting in frustration, anger, distrust, or resentment, but we still imagine we are supposed to wait until we're asked. We're still following the old idea of work. Once we break out of this old idea and start making carefully crafted, well-designed, thoughtful offers to others to whom we have listened carefully, we become more autonomous actors in our own story. We become contributors of value within our companies and position ourselves to innovate.

Recently I ran a program for senior-level leaders and their people. One particular session involved twenty people without their leaders, and one of the youngest participants asked an insightful question: "If I pursue this to its logical conclusion, does that mean that I get to be the actor, the designer, the instigator of my own work? Can I effectively become a free agent inside a company?" When you get masterful at crafting desirable offers, yes, you do. That doesn't mean you do whatever you want, however; it means you get to make any offer you want. Initially, your offers may not be accepted or considered valuable. However, as you become a more experienced and skilled listener, begin to pay more attention, and practice making offers, they will become progressively more valuable. Ultimately, they will be considered and appreciated.

Creating Customers

When we make an offer and that offer is accepted, we haven't just created a future. We've created a customer.

Typically, we think of a customer as someone who is buying something from someone. Within corporations, we've historically had bosses, not customers. But as we gain the new understanding of work, we discover that it is very effective to think of anyone who makes a request of you—including your boss—as your customer. It's even more effective to think of anyone you make an offer to as your customer. It changes the relationship of who can do what—and we have useful things like customer satisfaction, value, and service embedded in our consciousness when we think about a customer. Using the term *customer* inside a hierarchal organization facilitates a shift in our common sense around how we relate to our boss, project leader, or division head.

Most conversations at work today start with "Hey, can you do this for me?" And most performers rush into delivery mode, because that is how we have been trained from an early age. Remember homework? You did what you had been assigned and rarely had an opportunity to ask a question about it. That is the input-process-output model that we saw in chapter 1. Let's replace that model with a loop.

The Four Ds of Effective Work

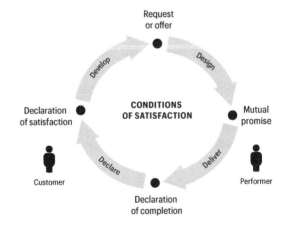

Credit: Adapted from Fernando Flores's *Conversations for Action and Collected Essays.*

This four-quadrant loop is a conversation between a customer (internal or external) and a performer. To start with, the customer needs to Develop a request that has sufficient richness and context for their performer to satisfy it, or the performer needs to listen to the customer and come to an understanding of their needs to Develop an offer that has sufficient richness and context.

Once the offer or request is accepted, the customer and performer together Design a clear understanding of what it will take to satisfy the customer. This is where the most powerful co-invention happens.

The third quadrant, Deliver, is where most of us are programmed to jump right to. We are always in a hurry to deliver, as if it's the most important part of the work. This is where our common sense tells us that the valuable work gets done. But this can also be the most wasteful part of work. If the Develop and Design conversations do not happen, there is a very high chance that the work will be off track—if circumstances change, the customer doesn't inform the performer, and consequently the customer will not Declare their satisfaction (quadrant four). Remember the last time you bust a gut doing some really great work only to jubilantly deliver it and discover that it was no longer needed? It's only when the customer Declares satisfaction that you move on to Develop a new request.

In the traditional input-process-output model of work, if somebody senior to you asks you to do something, you do it. But if that first step is instead a conversation, you can determine what way you want your work to go. As an input-process-output performer, if you change your priorities halfway through and decline to do the work or want to make a change, there are consequences. But if it is a conversation, you can make moves across the whole process to be more in charge of what's happening. And if you're the one who started the conversation—instead of receiving a request, you are making an offer—it changes everything in important ways.

In this new model, whenever you prepare an offer, design a mutual promise, and co-invent what it will take to satisfy them, you designate the person you have made the offer to as your customer, and you are the performer.

You can decide to whom you want to make offers; it could be anyone. Since offers build trust, you can decide with whom you want to build trust.

One of my innovation leadership development clients was very hesitant to consider two of the people he worked for as his customers. One of them was his direct line boss, and the other was the de facto head of the division. He felt uncomfortable with making them his customers as it seemed like a commercial, money-oriented interaction, more to do with an exchange of goods than innovation. So, since innovators are good at experimenting, I asked him to experiment and to see what happened when he said to one of his bosses, "I consider you to be my customer and I'm committed to delivering satisfaction for you as my customer, and I would like to do a review with you of my planned innovation strategy for my group."

The subtle and very important difference here is that he could have approached this review with the boss in the role of a teacher grading an assignment. Instead, when the person doing the review understands that they're the customer, they're committed to being satisfied with the outcome of the work, and the person having their innovation strategy reviewed understands that they are delivering satisfaction and value to the customer. The conversation moves closer to understanding the value of the research, how it will be applied, and how, ultimately, it could become technology transferred to a product development group. If the customer-performer relationship is set up early on, it facilitates a much deeper and richer conversation around value. And it also opens the door to create a higher level of trust, born from a commitment to satisfaction.

What would happen to your learning and your innovative capacity if you identified a new person, a new customer to make an offer to every quarter? What would happen to your influence and impact within your company? How would your understanding of your company's operations, strategy, customers, and position in the market expand?

Finding Effective Customers

In 2010, Derek Sivers did a fun and fabulous three-minute TED Talk (love those!) called "How to Start a Movement." Sivers is a musician, producer, circus performer, entrepreneur, TED speaker, and book publisher. If you get a chance, watch the video. Sivers shows his audience a video of a man dancing shirtless in a park: at first he's a lone nut, but then one person starts dancing as well, and that person, as Sivers says, "publicly shows everyone how to follow." Then a second person follows—and that's a turning point: "Three is a crowd and a crowd is news." More and more people join in, and it becomes easier and easier to join, and harder and harder not to join. But—and this is the key point—"it was the first follower that transformed a lone nut into a leader. There is no movement without the first follower."

What does that mean for us here? Without a customer, you are just another nut with a cool idea. To me, the most important part of Derek's speech is that "the leader embraces him as an equal, so it's not about the leader anymore—it's about them, plural." Your customer is the person who converts you from a lone nut into a cool person with a viable offer to innovate together. "If the leader is the flint, the first follower is the spark that makes the fire." That means you need the right first follower—the right customer. You need someone to engage in the full conversation with you, from offer to declaration of satisfaction.

This doesn't mean you should go dancing shirtless in the park. It means you should get savvy about finding effective customers.

An effective customer is someone who is:

- Committed and has skin in the game. Someone who has something to lose if the work is not successful, and something to gain if the work is successful.

- Capable of assessing the value of your work and helping you deliver satisfaction.

- Genuinely committed to being satisfied and ensuring that your work will be successful and impactful.

- Sincere in being satisfied with your offer. In other words, they will use their knowledge to help you craft something valuable to them and possibly to others.

- Involved in the work. They play some part in the delivery of the work and are committed to its successful completion.

Most importantly, an effective customer is someone with whom you want to build trust.

The legendary Terry Winograd himself is a good example of someone who reaped the benefit of good customers. In some sense, that is the majority of what the revolutionary computer science professor has! As Lawrence Fisher writes, "Winograd has no high-profile piece of technology to point to. In an age of software, it makes sense that his contributions are less tangible. He says his worldview is most visible in Google's many applications, not so much from his relatively brief tenure, but from the hundreds of his former students who work there. Many of them, he argues, have internalized his assumption that technology shouldn't just work on its own, but that it should work for and with people."

Larry Page, the cofounder of Google, is perhaps Winograd's most notable customer. It follows that Winograd has the some of the world's best customers. Establishing the Stanford Human-Computer Interaction Group required enough success and base of experience to garner support, and it also became a brilliant way for Winograd to nurture a base of committed, competent, and involved customers. For a long time, Winograd's ideas were unpopular and undervalued. However, Winograd accumulated influence as a public figure and consequently found the right kind of customers for his specific flavor of genius. The relationship between Larry Page and Terry Winograd can help show us what to look for in a committed and effective customer.

Effective Customer versus Task Assigner

Because of the nature of the hierarchical organizations that we work within, many of the people who assign work to us are program or project leads. They have lists of tasks that need to be completed, and we are often the people to whom these tasks get assigned.

Many times, the program and project leads are acting as intermediaries for more senior people who want to get work done. The problem with this is that we are removed one level of abstraction from those with the context to help us understand why we're doing what we're doing. If we apply the customer-performer model to this setup, either the program and project lead becomes the customer—in other words, they take the time to understand the context and conditions of satisfaction—or they become a performer for the more senior person who is perhaps managing a larger program. Understanding that allows us to retain the context, purpose, and value to be created as the requests get made down the chain.

Over time, as you start engaging in this customer and performer model, you will see your common sense shift: you will identify people who behave like customers. It doesn't matter what level of the organization they're in; they take the commitment and the responsibility of ensuring satisfaction. Because of that, they are better able to articulate the what, when, why, and how of requests they make. They're also able to engage with you as a performer in a way that brings your best knowledge and best co-invention capabilities to the work.

The Task Assigners versus Effective Customers table demonstrates the differences between someone who is simply moving things along—a paper pusher, checklist manager, or task assigner—and somebody who is committed to behaving like a customer inside an organization by ensuring satisfaction, articulating the conditions of satisfaction, and understanding context and value. Get good at identifying these people. When you do, you're already halfway to having effective customers for the offers that you want to make.

Task Assigners versus Effective Customers

Area	Task Assigners	Effective Customers
Leadership	Do their best to make it happen. May remain dissatisfied.	Commit to being satisfied. Is the customer for the success of the work (and for your success).
Satisfaction	Hope you tell them what you can deliver and may or may not be satisfied.	Know what will satisfy them. Do the work to know. Have their own standards, which they communicate.
Work commitment	Expect you to satisfy them—they will know if/when they see it.	Own their own satisfaction. Actively work with you to make that happen.
Customer-performer roles	You always work for them.	Sometimes they work for you, making offers to support you in your work for the team.
Commitment to you as a performer	Zero. Their job is to ask you to do things.	Committed to making sure you are successful.
Changes	Adapt as best they can. Aim to let you know as things change—if they remember.	Seek to give you as much context as possible. Update you as context and circumstances change. Work with you to renegotiate your shared commitment as circumstances change and you both develop a more sophisticated understanding of the work.
Vision	You are charged with implementing their external vision.	Own the vision—which is often their own and aligns with that of the company.

Training Someone to Be Your Customer

I have found that few people are good at being customers inside companies. Once I find someone willing to be my customer, I have to train them to be effective in the role. What does that mean? The most important thing to remember here is that as much as you're unused to having a customer, they're unused to being a customer.

I find it effective to train someone to be your customer by *telling them* that they're your customer, and that you're committed to satisfying them in the particular work you're doing for them. That's immediately a shock for them, and often they'll ask you for clarification. The answer is that you're interested in co-designing and/or co-inventing with them. What does it take for this to work?

There's a trap here that you need to be careful of. I had a terrific guy on a team that I was leading, and he would come into my office and ask, "What can I do to help?" I eventually realized why I was getting so frustrated with what seemed like a very nice offer: he wasn't doing the thinking to figure out what to offer. He was relying on me to bridge what I was trying to accomplish, the strategies that needed to be executed, the people that needed to be managed, or the budgets that needed to be prepared. He was expecting me to identify where he fit in all that. It would have been much more effective if he had said, "I've been at your meetings and paying attention for the last month, and I think that there's a particular area where I can offer value. Would you mind if I sat down to talk to you about it?" I would have been delighted to effectively co-invent the conditions of satisfaction: what it would take for him to deliver that offer to me, and what it would mean for me to be satisfied with it.

Whenever you're making an offer and designating a more senior person as your customer, do enough homework to ensure your offer is strong. Make sure that you are in a position to design the conditions of satisfaction with them. (I will go into more detail about this later in this book.) The important thing to remember is to come to the table having done some pretty solid design around what you think is an appropriate, effective, timely, valuable, and trust-building offer for your potential customer.

In preparing your offer, do yourself a favor and design your own and your customers' standards for satisfaction—with your customer. In order to design commitments in a dynamic environment, we must learn to create alignment. Designing shared standards pledges trust with the other person.

In preparing your offer, it is also important to design what *your* standards are for satisfaction. How will you know when you've done your rock-star best, and how do you codesign that with your customer? (We'll explore that in chapter 4.)

Key Practice: Template for Effective Offers

Designing effective offers is an important starting point for co-invention. Using the Language/Action Perspective can help make your offers more effective. This framework for crafting effective offers is based on the principles of the LAP. By following this template, you can create an offer that is an invitation to co-invent rather than a "take it or leave it" done deal. Additionally, using the Language/Action Perspective helps you addresses the concerns of your customer in your offer.

Step 1: Set the Context
We understand the importance of context in the world around us. It's just as important to creating shared understanding

with potential internal customers—those people who might accept your offer. In order to craft our best offers, it's essential to create a common context for shared understanding. From this shared understanding, we will co-invent effective conditions of satisfaction with our customers. This is the first step in establishing a framework for how we'll work together.

Topic	Why it is important for context
Theme	What is the area/subject matter of the big problem you are offering to solve?
Project	What is the title of your project?
Customer	Who understands your offer and is committed to being an effective customer?
Performer(s)	• You • Team

Step 2: Build and Confirm Shared Understanding

What are the business issues?
What's not working?
How are these issues affecting people's lives?

(Note: Quotes from individuals struggling with the problem are useful here.)

Step 3: Clarify the Value Proposition

If we succeed at this, what do we gain?

- ○ Money
- ○ Time
- ○ Happiness
- ○ Status

Step 4: Establish the Metrics for Impact

- ○ Establish a baseline
- ○ Current cycle time
- ○ Data throughput
- ○ Data quality
- ○ Model performance

Timeline

Phasing your project is a highly effective way to scope your offers. It provides multiple opportunities to build trust with your customer and helps you manage the conditions of satisfaction in increments. Specify date ranges for each phase of the timeline.

- Phase 1
- Phase 2
- Phase 3
- Bringing it all together: Mapping the total project duration
- Case study and metrics

Commitments

- What will I and/or my team commit to?
- What will the customer commit to?
- What do we want our supporters to commit to?

Risk Factors: Breakdown in Trust

A breakdown in trust is always a risk, but we can design very effective ways to mitigate it. How do you design your project, engagement, communications, and concerns so as to be constantly building rather than destroying trust?

Questions for Clarification

To co-invent with your customer:

- Who on your team should be involved in this conversation?
- Do we want to explore a Plan B?

Retrospective

- Looking back at our goals, what did we accomplish?
- What was the impact?

3

Power and Commitments

or, Inventing a Better Future

---

*"Tell me and I forget. Teach me and
I remember. Involve me and I learn."*
CHINESE APHORISM

ARGARET THATCHER got her nickname "the Iron Lady" in part because of her determination to crush the UK's trade unions. The unions responded with strikes and labor actions in the winter of 1978–79, and strikes, shortages, and general civil disquiet continued well into the mid-'80s when I was in college in London. I remember the piles of trash in black bags on every corner. Union members were working—they were just "working to rule": they did no more than the minimum required by the rules of their contracts, and they precisely followed all safety and other regulations.

Of course, this caused a slowdown and decrease in productivity: they were no longer working during breaks, unpaid extended hours, or on weekends, and—most importantly—they were not using their intelligence and local knowledge to do their work expertly. They were complying, following to the letter the rules imposed on them, top-down, by bosses and bureaucrats. Waste collectors were doing their work the way someone higher up in the organization chart, tucked away in some office, thought they should be doing it. And it was a disaster. It showed the massive difference between someone doing something because they're told to do it and someone making a personal commitment to do something. Individual intelligence, know-how, and motivation matter if we want things to run smoothly, let alone if we want to innovate.

And yet we still believe that bosses should set rules and employees should follow them, just like Henry Ford's assembly-line workers did. As managers, we can get trapped in arrogance when we think we can tell someone what to do, down to the minutiae of their daily tasks. We have all learned, over the years, that this style of management is expected and accepted, even if we also know how bad it can feel. When we work in the realm of having power over people, we push them into the death knell of innovation: malicious compliance. Instead of team cocreation, we get mounds of black plastic trash bags.

In chapter 1, I talked about building yourself as an observer, practicing observation and observing common sense. In chapter 2, I introduced you to the powerful practice of making courageous offers and commitments. In this chapter, we will dig more deeply into what it means to make commitments: why they are so powerful within organizations and how they can impact your ability to do amazing work while leading people. We will explore the dynamics of power and autonomy that can move a company away from malicious compliance towards successful delivery. And we will explore co-invention—not just making offers and commitments to one other person, but innovating collectively as a team, among ourselves, and with our customers. We are developing an understanding of work as a network of commitments. We'll see how to grow and manage people through a deeper understanding of commitments, and how to inform and guide this through the right kind of listening to drive innovation and value.

Manage Commitments, Lead People

The world of work is in transformation. Who we work with and how work looks and feels is radically different than even half a decade ago. Many of our tools are new. Much of the change has been evolutionary, but these rapid shifts offer us an opportunity to intentionally redesign our systems and structures: to move away from the old-school, top-down, input-process-output model of work to the new cocreative vision of work we saw in chapter 1. It's a shift that's long overdue; although it might seem to be a product of our twenty-first-century world, it was first described before our bosses were born, back when Henry Ford was running his factories, by Mary Parker Follett.

Born in 1868 in Massachusetts, Mary Parker Follett worked as a management consultant on the East Coast in the early 1900s. She offered the world of work a new way to engage. She pointed out the lateral structures of commitment within otherwise hierarchical organizations, firms, and institutions. In demonstrating how employees were already collaborating and using nonhierarchical workflows to get things done, she created a new understanding of management potential.

At the time, many in the field of public management were focused on mechanization, industrialization, and formal organizational aspects of work. Task tracking, procedures, and power-over hierarchy were the norm. This perspective fueled much of the growth of a young administrative state, and to its credit, it formed a strong institutional foundation for the US civil service infrastructure, which was progressive in the early 1900s. But we now know that neither governments nor corporations succeed for long because of task tracking, procedures, and power-over hierarchy—sometimes quite the opposite. Organizations succeed because of the ingenuity and agility of the people within them, and Follett tapped into that. She made lasting contributions in several areas:

- *Diversity*: Follett understood well the impact of diversity on organizational productivity and innovation. At a time when power-over was the practice of the day, she called for bringing out a variety of ideas and perspectives in group sessions. The practice was designed to ensure that the best approach emerged.

- *Lifelong learning:* Follett was primarily an educator. She considered education to be the lifeblood of knowledge, innovation, and improvement, at the organizational and individual levels. Her vision laid the foundation for adult learning and knowledge creation as we understand it today.

- *Engagement:* Follett was a strong advocate of engagement: the strength of the mental and emotional connection employees feel towards the work they do, their teams, and their organization. She considered discourse regarding shared experiences, humble inquiry, and a search for meaning to be the pathways to learning and improvement. Follett knew that getting a diverse group of people engaged with one another was a powerful force.

- *The human element:* Follett viewed humans, not procedures, as the most valuable part of an organization. She was one of the earliest voices to argue for the value of positive organizational culture and the importance of placing people first.

These ideas were unheard of in Follett's time. We are still not very good at implementing them in our own time. The practices that she espoused a century ago are the foundation for a lot of the transformation leadership work done today. But we have much more transformation still to do, and we are in a time when we can and must make it happen.

Power and Autonomy

The shift in mindset from managing people to managing a network of commitments offers an opportunity for better leadership and mutual investment in shared outcomes. You don't manage people; you manage commitments—your own and those of your team. The Power/Autonomy Model is a useful way to understand this: what to do and what not to do. The x-axis distinguishes between tracking tasks and managing commitments, and the y-axis distinguishes between power-over and power-with people. The interactions of these four values give us four different project management modes.

The Power/Autonomy Model

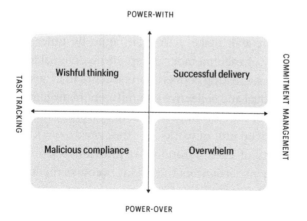

The notion of power-over stems from belief that the leader knows best, has all the answers about what needs to happen, and can tell everyone what to do because they have ultimate authority over their staff's future at work. In fact, they know enough to define and document each member of their team's work, down to the last task.

Power-with is a simple concept but hard to implement. It is an honest acknowledgment of the glaring fact that even though you are the fearless leader, you do not always (or even usually) know best, you do not have all the answers, and you do not know enough about what needs to happen to tell everyone what to do. You recognize that your power comes through working *with* your team.

Task tracking operates on the assumption that the individual executing a given task has neither responsibility nor interest in the overall outcome. This thinking makes perfect sense if you are setting up work structures around production-related jobs, where each step and skill is discrete, and the focus is purely on output. Although almost all of our project management approaches are based on task tracking, am I right in guessing that you can see how at odds this is with power-with? Task tracking treats workers as parts in an input-process-output machine. "But how else do I make sure work is done and remains agile?" Everything I'm talking about here will make your team agile by unleashing the autonomy of each member to tap into individual and collective genius, creating cooperation rather than chaos.

Individual and collective commitment management are at the heart of the new understanding of work. Commitments are the fractal unit of work—in other words, work builds on the efforts of each autonomous individual. Commitment management recognizes this and it becomes the foundation of a new understanding of our individual and collective roles at work and in society. It acknowledges that we amplify each other's brilliance. It acknowledges we are autonomous but deeply interconnected; we own our own work; we innovate better together.

Now let's look at the modes these four values create in interaction.

Malicious Compliance

Malicious compliance is the intersection of task tracking and power-over: it happens when people do what they are *forced* to do. (See graphic on page 63.)

Malicious compliance arises when employees are constrained in their actions, are limited in their roles, lack autonomy, and are pushed into doing their work in a limited way. Required reporting tasks like annual evaluations, financial reporting, or status updates tend to trigger this attitude. Rather than seeing these tasks as an opportunity to grow and influence the workplace around us, because we are obliged to complete them, many of us approach them from the perspective of malicious compliance. We haven't yet recognized that in doing so we make them more onerous and difficult for ourselves.

Malicious compliance presents a negative set of possible outcomes for workplace environments and is symptomatic of management issues. Employees who do their work but are frustrated by the power-over structure and the helicopter-parent approach to task management are more likely to work less smoothly. The task-driven, top-down nature of this management system is familiar to most who work in a group.

Over the years, I have found that the people who have an understanding of the tremendous influence they can have across the organization—a sense of the power they can have and the commitments to others—somehow approach these "chores" from the perspective of joy. In doing that, they make it easier to complete their necessary tasks and to begin a new task next time. The negative emotional weight is alleviated, and the task seems less distasteful in the future. You might feel under the gun and obliged to do something that is compliance-related, but ask yourself, "Do I want to feel like a Thatcher-era garbage collector, or do I want to approach this with a perspective of creating influence and make it easier to deliver on what is being requested of me?"

One of my coaching clients is working in the middle of a broken financial reporting process. It takes two hours of each of her people's time every single month. She has many other external deadlines bearing down on her at the same time. I encouraged her to begin a conversation with the CFO: "I am committed to delivering full transparency of my organization, my allocation of people, and how it is we're using our budgets. However, in the absence of what I need from you, I can't deliver on that commitment. Can you please help me?" She is demonstrating her commitment to building and maintaining trust with her CFO. She knows they need to calibrate to serve that trust, and if they can do that, she'll work more effectively with a lot less time wasted. She's both expressing that she's frustrated with the existing process and making it plain that she is committed to delivering on her existing reporting commitments. She's opening a space of deep trust.

Mary Parker Follett was prescient in anticipating the organizational flows of the world we now live in. Knowledge work demands and benefits from a more dynamic and flexible approach, with a human focus. As we move away from the item-driven, task-specific, top-down work of the past, it makes no sense to apply old logic to new work patterns, relationships, and environments. New management strategies are essential as we progress!

Wishful Thinking

Wishful thinking happens when you have a partnership (power-with), but instead of real commitment, you are tracking all the issues and tasks (task tracking). (See graphic on page 63.) The result is painful and makes successful delivery very elusive.

Wishful thinking can happen when an organization has dissolved some of its task tracking, but neither leadership nor team members have mastered the new and necessary challenge of clearly constructed commitments. This can result in an excess of enthusiastic commitment: everyone is excited about doing the work they find most compelling and are best equipped to do, but old task-tracking mentalities get in the way. Without new strategies and practices for managing and developing solid commitments and shared standards, wishful thinking takes over. There is a sense that everything is going well, and yet, somehow, nothing effective is happening.

It is only by digging below the wishful thinking that we can get to real commitments. It requires a deep understanding of commitments and how to weave these into every conversation, every contract, every customer meeting, every project plan, and every support agreement—and, most importantly, how to know when they are missing. The people you engage with at work offer a complex array of skills and abilities. Honoring each person's unique abilities within the chain of commitment-building sounds daunting, but it offers unexpected flexibility and benefit.

A few years ago, I had a delightful client whom I was working with to create and align objectives and key results (OKRs). He decided the most effective way to lead his team in engaging people in the OKR process—which at times can feel very top-down—was to start from mastery. (We will talk about mastery more in chapter 5.) To accomplish this, he asked each individual to identify their areas of mastery as well as the areas they were particularly interested in working in or pursuing growth and understanding in over the next year. Then he matched that with what he knew the company was interested in doing. His team had conversations about how their interests fit into the overall research direction of the organization. He ended up with OKRs that people had made genuine commitments to and were more indicative of what they actually cared about. And they were completely transparent: every person on the team knew what mattered to each other, how that related to their personal pursuit of mastery, and what they had committed to accomplish over the next year. This also set them up to help each other by making offers, which amplified the innovation capacity of the team as measured by their new technical capability delivery to the company.

These OKRs were not a result of begrudgingly made commitments the team members thought would make money for the company, but which ignored or compromised their own innovation drive and interests. In this case, because of this practice, both their own interests and the company's desire to produce innovative products aligned very nicely. The level of commitment he got from his team as a result was significant, as were his chances of delivering on his OKRs. In addition, the calibration and recalibration the team was able to do—because they had made personal commitments to these OKRs, which were clearly owned by named individuals—meant there was a lot less noise-to-signal ratio, and a lot less strife in the inevitable dance of coordination over the subsequent year.

Leaders are granted credibility to make decisions, organize projects, and make large-scale commitments. They are expected to be reliable, so they might hesitate to renegotiate the power structures embedded within the organization. When your role is to imagine all potential outcomes, good and bad, altering the chain of command may seem risky. Leaders operate within a network of commitments that can be verbal, direct, or recorded in an OKR or project plan. Managing these well is integral to completing projects successfully. The solution is to offer employees, coworkers and team members the opportunity to design, negotiate, make, manage, and keep their commitments. This empowers everyone to a degree of design and a higher level of personal ownership. Individuals are more likely to invest in their work when they have the autonomy to make, design, negotiate, and even decline commitments.

Yes, even decline. Declining means a commitment *not* to do something that still leaves the other person knowing where they stand. How often do you wish someone had had the autonomy and integrity to say no, rather than leave you in wishful thinking? Amplifying people's level of ownership and involvement in crafting the work they deliver facilitates this sort of identification. Saying no at work demands an awareness of prior commitments and a strong sense of priority. It can be helpful to notice who is active in saying no. Often, these actors are in positions of power or feel empowered to refuse work that doesn't align with their overarching commitments. If you consider an old boss (particularly someone who was effective), it is probably easy to recall an instance when they refused something—an offer, an extra project, or a request from an employee. Sometimes these noes are frustrating or demonstrate a person's desire to flex authority; however, some degree of refusal is integral in completing what is already at play. Without being able to decline, you have no ability to make clean, honest commitments and you have limited ability to prioritize.

The space between a power-with organizational structure and a commitment-based management strategy allows for successful delivery by team members and leaders. When good leadership becomes synonymous with power-with and recognizes the negative outcomes associated with power-over, leadership means managing the networked commitments of your team members.

Overwhelm

A few years ago, I was working for one of America's largest banks. Its loan document processing group was struggling with what seemed to be an issue of inefficiency, and the bank was losing both deals and customers at an alarming rate.

There were two very different groups on either side of the loan sales process, and these two groups did not know how best to communicate with one another, how to manage their shared commitments, or how to operate beyond a task-tracking focus. The commercial bankers, who were predominantly white middle-class men and college-educated, struggled to dialogue successfully with the document processors, who were predominantly women of color with high-school diplomas who had learned English as a second language. The two sides existed inside different networks of concerns.

Both groups were frustrated by what they saw as the shortcomings of the other group, which impacted performance, communication, morale, and ultimately the division's ability to innovate solutions. A lack of practice and empathy kept pushing these two groups apart, preventing them from collaborating and innovating. There was no preexisting structure that allowed the document processors to decline work. They felt obligated to take on everything assigned to them— or lobbed over the wall at them—which produced a top-down power-over dynamic and they lived in overwhelm.

One of the crucial elements of the commitment-driven approach is teaching and encouraging team members and leaders how and when to say no, as doing so can be difficult and even frowned upon. Work culture often expects us to take on as many tasks and responsibilities as possible. Encouraging coworkers to make offers and engage in designing their network of commitments without offering the equal opportunity to decline can lead to overwhelm. Overwhelm happens when people feel forced to make commitments. (See graphic on page 63.) A forced commitment is not a real commitment and will soon unravel—and will often revert to malicious compliance or burnout.

Most of us are optimistic about the amount of work we can complete, but when given the opportunity to design more of our work, enthusiasm can override a practical sense of what is manageable: our eyes get bigger than our schedules. The underlying pressure of work culture to complete as much work as possible also contributes to overwhelm. Shifting the balance of power alone is not always enough. To arrive at successful delivery, we must understand how good commitments are made and managed.

If what you are doing right now is task tracking and you do not have real, documented commitments that form the critical path of your projects, which allow and support people saying no, you are not on track for success. Shifting the balance of power between managers and team members towards a power-with approach de-emphasizes task tracking. Successful delivery requires a clear network of commitments that drive and orient the work. Understanding our capacities, what community offers we can make, and when and how to say no becomes more important when we design and manage more of what we do at work. Taking on too much can lead to overwork and burnout, and to the same kind of resentment that task tracking is likely to produce: we become frustrated and even buried by the freedom and flexibility we previously found so interesting.

Cultivating the permission to say no within your team doesn't create negativity; it more appropriately directs positive energy and workplace optimism. People rarely flat-out say a complete no to each other, except in extreme circumstances. Optimally, we cultivate an environment where team members can make a counteroffer, a request for clarity, or a request for a design session.

Let's say you make a request of somebody on your team, but you're in a hurry and the request is somewhat incomplete. The team member comes back to you an hour later and says, "I've done some thinking and research around this, and I can't commit to doing it. Can I sit down with you for ten minutes to understand better what it is that you're looking for?" In a sense, they have declined your request, but they felt comfortable enough to make a counteroffer. In these moments, you can have some of your best design conversations. You have someone who cares and wants to make a commitment and who is not feeling coerced into making a commitment. This practice produces a higher degree of successful delivery and moves you out of power-over.

Successful Delivery

Successful delivery is what you get when power-with and commitment management work together (see graphic on page 63), and it's what this book is about—and what we're going to keep looking at in depth. It requires clear conditions of satisfaction and a developed network of trust. Clear conditions of satisfaction allow for trust inside work. For example, to do your best work, you must understand what sort of "best work" is imagined, necessary, and relevant. This means clearly fleshing out the conditions of satisfaction before making a commitment, and then using discernment to occasionally say no when the conditions aren't right.

Successful delivery also means constant interaction. It means that, as a leader, you're not just reaping the value produced by your people; you're actively involved in growing them.

Grow People

Common sense tells us that leadership is about intervening when there are problems or breakdowns. It's about raising awareness for people when we believe we are out of alignment with strategy, discussing alternatives and different ways of doing things, establishing goals, building trust, and setting standards. These are effective (and we will discuss them in depth in chapter 4), but they are not enough on their own.

Understanding the Power/Autonomy Model offers insight into how to grow people. I know that developing an environment of power-with and commitment management is more conducive to agility, flexibility, resilience—and innovation.

Old Common Sense	New Common Sense
Intervening	Enabling others to invent more valuable narratives for themselves by:
Raising Awareness	Making, keeping, and asking for commitments
Discussing Alternatives	Co-inventing solutions
Establishing Goals	Creating goals based on shared ambitions
Setting Standards	Establishing shared standards

When we move into power-with leadership, we create a context for facilitating people's growth. Our main job as leaders becomes enabling others to invent more valuable narratives and more valuable futures together. We do this by helping them make, keep, request, and manage commitments to take action based on specific standards. As leaders, we also build our capacity to do this by observing the limits of other people's perspectives; we accommodate them with compassion and by establishing shared standards that we co-invent together. This lets us evolve, design, and raise those standards over time.

One of the most effective ways I have found to accomplish this is to harness the power of delegation towards the purpose of growing people. Instead of delegation being a top-down approach—I give you work to do, and you do it no questions asked because I am the boss—it becomes a very powerful tool for growing people. My rule of thumb for this is simple:

> If someone can do something 75 percent as well as you can, request that they do it, and coach them through or serve them for the remaining 25 percent.

I remember a colleague of mine in a consulting firm pulling me aside and politely telling me that I was making a big mistake. She had seen that I was allowing my people to make requests of me to help them deliver on work I had asked them to do. She advised me that this was very damaging and would do me harm as a leader. This has so long been a practice of mine for growing people that it took me awhile to understand what she was talking about. She was pointing out that I was stepping outside the power-over paradigm (which she automatically accepted). She was unaware of the fact that I was using it as a tool to grow my people.

If you're deeply committed to growing your people—in other words, if you're smart enough to want clever people to make offers to take things off your plate so you can lead them to do things they never thought were possible together—then request that they do work for you that it is 25 percent above their capacity. Offer to be the performer in certain parts to support them in delivering to you as the customer, and you coach to the 25 percent.

Let me give you a simple example. I have a wonderful guy on my team who does a lot of our tech support and helps us architect new systems to support our clients. I asked him to build an online version of an assessment that we offer. He'd never done something like that before. I gave him full responsibility to do it—but I also offered to be his performer for testing the assessment and ensuring that other team members, who are his peers, also did some early testing. I became a performer in his network of commitments, and I treated him as the customer. In the bigger commitment, I was his customer, but this commitment allowed me to work with him both as a performer and as a customer, giving him a level of authority and autonomy in a subset of the project which he would not otherwise have had.

When you teach people how to be effective customers and you also teach them that being a customer is not always easy, they become much more proficient in negotiating and designing the conditions that will satisfy the customer, and they become much more respectful and appreciative of your job as the customer for most of the work done by your team. It builds a level of trust that allows for growth over time. And to be entirely practical here, it means that you are systematically growing people who will take stuff off your plate. I'm a fan of that.

Committing to growing people stretches our abilities and moves us from leadership as administration to leadership as enabling. And we don't give up power by sharing it with others. We still take the lead in working with others to design and advance strategy, and we continue to introduce and instill our vision within the organization. But we no longer need to have all the answers, exclusively develop blueprints, set goals, or intervene when those goals are not met to our satisfaction. We are leading a group of autonomous individuals to create something bigger together than they thought was possible alone.

The essence of inventing a better future is in a skill set that requires us to use our intelligence, capability, and perspective alongside others.

Sustaining Successful Delivery

Why do we find tennis such a fantastic game to watch? And why does doubles tennis sometimes make for a more dynamic match?

Many of us who have played tennis know that it's a cooperative and collaborative game. If you get permission to coach your practice partner, you can up their game while upping your own. The better you practice with your practice partner, the better the game. You're relying on both of you to embody the rules, use the tools and the practices, and play a better and better game. In the same way, when every person on your team plays the game of managing and making commitments, you all can become more creative and ideally also more innovative.

Increasing the autonomous capability of your people while making room for them to say no demands that you level up your own leadership. Leading from a position of commitment-based management puts you in a place of continuous learning because you're working in a system of continuous feedback loops. And so the return on your effort is exponential: you've set up a game in which you can continuously grow while growing the capability of your team.

Key to this approach is listening to other people and understanding what matters to them. It's similar to how you would listen to your tennis partner and understand what their strengths and weaknesses are in the game. When you listen to what matters to other people, you learn how they play the game and how, in partnership with them, you are able to play an ever better game.

Fernando Flores introduced me to a powerful and effective way of what he referred to as "listening for concerns." I've come to think of this as listening for opportunities to co-invent and innovate with others. It's a simple ladder of people's ongoing concerns. Start at the bottom of the ladder, and you can begin to listen for—and pay attention to—what immediately matters to others.

Breakdowns

What is staring your customer in the face? What's front of mind for them? These are usually their breakdowns—the stuff that is not working in their lives—at work, in their research, or in their innovation. Their breakdowns preoccupy them and keep them in a state of coping rather than creating.

When I was a kid, I went to Catholic school (for my sins). Every year, just before Easter, the nuns would team up with a national charity to raise money for children starving in Africa. Why were nuns focusing on food rather than—as they were with us—teaching the children about God? Because they knew, from experience, that you can't teach people if they're hungry. Before they could "educate" the children of Africa about Christ, the children needed to be fed. Breakdowns are much the same. You can't innovate with people under stress or in a panic.

Listening for Concerns

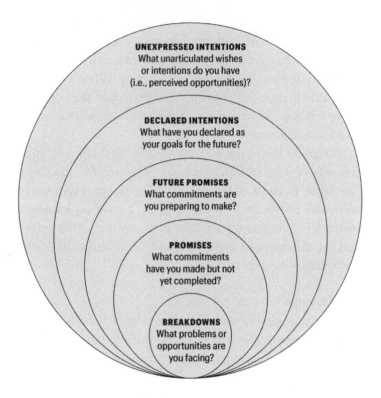

UNEXPRESSED INTENTIONS
What unarticulated wishes
or intentions do you have
(i.e., perceived opportunities)?

DECLARED INTENTIONS
What have you declared as
your goals for the future?

FUTURE PROMISES
What commitments are
you preparing to make?

PROMISES
What commitments
have you made but not
yet completed?

BREAKDOWNS
What problems or
opportunities are
you facing?

Breakdowns happen at work because of poor communication, bad infrastructure, unclear process, or inattentive
leadership. These are our most basic concerns at work. These
are the issues that seem to arise on repeat. Breakdowns are the
work-related equivalent of missing your dentist appointment
because your car stopped running—either your teenager left
the overhead light on and ran down the battery, or something
inexplicable happened and suddenly you're stranded on the
shoulder of the highway. One of these scenarios is the result
of poor communication and bad commitment management,

and the other one is part of a random and unpredictable life, but both are breakdowns. Our customers might articulate these concerns directly or indirectly, and they're exactly the sort of thing we should be listening for. If you're interested in co-inventing or innovating with somebody, help them deal with their broken stuff first and then move beyond it. It's a hugely effective way of building trust. And since trust is the foundation of all innovation, it's a very good place to start. If people don't trust you, they're not going to create knowledge with you.

Promises

Everyone makes promises and commitments to others. Some of us keep these promises in our minds, on to-do lists, in project plans, or on sticky notes. With the pace of work today, most of us live in a constant state of managing breakdowns and promises—otherwise referred to as coping.

Breakdowns happen when promises don't go according to plan. Which happens often. We all have promises that we are working on. Whether those promises are in breakdown, and we are still struggling to complete them, or whether they are going according to plan, we still own them, manage them, coordinate around them, and seek to deliver on them.

Future Promises

Future promises are slightly different. They are commitments you are preparing to make—for something you care deeply about or have already made a bigger commitment to. They might show up as objectives and key results, retirement planning, saving for college, or paying off a mortgage.

Once we pay attention to our own future promises, we begin to attune ourselves to the future promises of our teammates, customers, and colleagues. We get better at negotiating promises with them, which are better aligned with our own and others' workloads and are more respectful of our own and others' time. We get more adept at doing the dance of coordinating with others.

Declared Intentions

Declared intentions have more to do with goals. You are committed but have not yet operationalized them. They are clear ambitions for the future—longer-term ambitions that you have shared with a few others, perhaps your partner, colleagues, or your boss. For example, a few years ago, my declared intention was to write a book. I subsequently did; in fact, this is my second. Declaring your intentions focuses your energy and opens the door for others to help you. Declared intentions may show up in your five- or ten-year plan and are certainly something you have discussed with your co-invention partner at work or in your personal life.

When someone does you the honor of sharing their declared intentions with you, they are inviting you to understand them and what matters to them at a level far beyond the usual chitchat. They are positioning you to make offers to them and build trust with them. Learn to recognize and appreciate it for what it is: an invitation to a deeper level of co-invention.

Unexpressed Intentions

Unexpressed intentions are the most fun! They are what your brain, heart, and soul are reaching towards, yet you may not even have language to put around them. They may be an emerging vision on the periphery of your hopes, wishes, and dreams. These are so important and so much fun to articulate with another human being. Doing so is deeply trust-building because it requires a tremendous amount of vulnerability, introspection, self-revelation, and sharing mutual appreciation. These are your secrets and aspirations, and when somebody listens and hears well enough to articulate them with you, it is an act of honor, respect, and deep appreciation.

In the context of offers, these make you an invaluable partner or co-inventor. We all want someone who can draw out our magnificence and our aspirations through the acts of listening and co-invention. If and when you get good at these, then co-inventing and innovating is only limited by your ability to find others willing to explore these unchartered territories with you. Practice making offers (and refer back to chapter 2), and over time you will get better and better at listening and co-invention.

Listening for Autonomy

The most effective thing you can do when seeking to innovate with another person is to listen. When you learn how to listen and take the practice seriously, you open yourself up to a greater level of co-invention than you thought possible.

When we align the power and autonomy model with listening for concerns, we also save time and energy. Invariably, when we are working with a customer or delivering work within our team, a natural drift occurs—our concerns change over time. As the year goes on, for example, I develop a better understanding of what I'm delivering for my customers. As global circumstances change, as I read new documents, as I become more knowledgeable in my area of innovation or research, requests that I've made (or commitments someone made to me) change a little. They become more or less relevant and urgent. By consistently listening to other people's concerns and tuning into those concerns as they grow and mature, we are better able to calibrate and recalibrate our commitments.

Making these adjustments to our commitments through the practice of strategic listening is where true agility comes from. Strategic listening is the foundation for a long-term relationship with a customer, whatever sort of customer, in which we become progressively more valuable to them. The Trust and Value Ladder shows the relationship between listening for what matters to others and anticipating requests and making innovative offers to them.

The Trust and Value Ladder

Build Trust and Value		
If you have the courage to	You will	You will be
Make innovative offers	Co-invent to satisfy unexpressed intentions	Trusted and invaluable
Make offers	Satisfy declared intentions	In partnership
Anticipate requests	Make useful promises	Appreciated
Destroy Trust		
Only respond to requests	Create breakdowns	Outsourceable

Remember: you can only make offers as big as the trust you have built. This is true whether you're in a leadership position or you're developing an offer with someone above you at work. Cultivating a power-with work environment allows for a more dynamic workflow. Power-with requires us to be proactive in managing our network of commitments. Alignment, continuous improvement, and sustained successful delivery are all outgrowths of commitment management and strategic listening. Practices for listening to concerns allow us to innovate at work. Innovation is made possible by the types of dynamic delivery we hope to engage at work. In the next chapter, we will look at how this gets applied cross-functionally.

Key Practice: Listening for Concerns to Make Offers, Build Trust, and Co-Invent

This key practice is a set of group activities. You can't learn to listen without someone to listen to, after all. They're taken from my Next Level Innovations Leaders program; one of the practices we focus on is helping leaders master co-invention for innovation.

Conversation Timeline
- Activity 1: Listening to Build Trust: 10 minutes
- Activity 2: Listening for Concerns: 25 minutes
- Activity 3: Trust and Innovation: 15 minutes
- Activity 4: Wrap Up and Action Steps: 10 minutes

Activity 1: Listening to Build Trust
Required time: 10 minutes
Required supplies: Whiteboard and markers
Note to Conversation Leaders: The group may come to the practice with the idea that listening is a light topic, particularly

if they've only skimmed this chapter. Be ready to share your own thoughts on how the Power/Autonomy Model created new insights for you, or key issues that need to be addressed within the group. This will be helpful if some participants underestimate the importance of this topic.

Prep Work
Each person should come to the conversation having read this chapter. An additional pre-read suggestion is the *Harvard Business Review* article "The Neuroscience of Trust."

Introduction for the Group
Put the following in your own words:

- As we co-invent outcomes with colleagues and customers and create mutual conditions of satisfaction, we need new interpretations and a new level of listening.

- Trust is woven deeply through this work, and by listening for concerns, we can better attune our offers to meet customer concerns and to build trust and partnership.

- It's critical that through our interactions, we listen deeply for our own interpretations of the world and for our customers' interpretations.

- As we do this, we move from asserting our ideas and towards co-inventing. This means saying less of "It needs to be this way" and more of "What comes up for me... How does that sit with you? Is there another option to consider?"

- We also move into a powerful place of inquiry when we are conversing and listening to more deeply understand customer concerns: what matters to them; what they stand for in the world; how they want to be seen, heard, and valued; what they want to accomplish and be known for; what their preferences are for how they prefer to work.

- We also need to consider the neuroscience of trust. There are physiological changes in the brain that trigger deeper trust.

Questions for the Group (3–5 minutes)
- What resonated most for you in the reading materials?

- It's really easy to take a superficial "blah, blah building trust" attitude to the topic of listening and trust. Why is it an important topic for us to explore?

- How do you feel about the concept of listening to build trust? What came to mind about trust levels in your roles, interactions, and work as you read the materials?

Activity 2: Listening for Concerns
Required time: 25 minutes
Required supplies: Pen, paper, whiteboard, and markers
Note to Conversation Leaders: The goal in this activity is to help the group understand that their ability to listen for concerns is critical in building trust with customers. You'll want to put a two-column chart on the whiteboard (or flipchart) that has "Customers" at the top of the left column and "Concerns Examples" at the top of the right column.

Introduction for the Group
Put the following in your own words:

- We're going to dive into the topic of trust breakdowns. We'll explore what exactly listening for concerns would be like (what we say, how it feels) to understand how it might change the relationship and trust within it.

Questions to Discuss as a Full Group (10–15 minutes)

- Let's talk about situations where we see trust is breaking down—whether we're the customer or the performer.

- Where is this happening? *(Write these answers on the whiteboard in the left column.)*

- To increase trust by listening for concerns, what would we say to convey and achieve a deeper level of listening? *(Write these answers in the right column; you may need to remind the group to reserve judgment here.)*

- If you read the *HBR* article "The Neuroscience of Trust," what else would you do or say to trigger a greater sense of trust for the customer? What would that feel like for the customer? For the performer?

- If this happened in every interaction you had with customers (including colleagues who make requests of you), how would this change your relationships with them? Would you benefit?

- Is this difficult to do? Why?

Questions to Discuss in Pairs (5–10 minutes)

- Where is trust an issue in your relationships, personal or professional?

- Where will you start to apply the concept of listening for concerns? Will this be difficult for you to do?

Questions to Discuss as a Full Group (3–5 minutes)

- Do you any comments about the situations you discussed? *(Share only to the level people are comfortable with.)*

Activity 3: Trust and Innovation

Required time: 15 minutes

Introduction for the Group

Put the following in your own words:

- If we want to work our way up in the Trust and Value Ladder, we need to consider how to use the concerns or additional observations from the discussions to change our offers.

- If greater innovation is our goal, we may need to ask different questions, relay our understanding back to the customer, and potentially change how we offer them solutions (in ways that reinforce that we have heard them).

- We're going to apply the listening for concerns skills we just discussed to situations where increased innovation is the goal.

Questions to Discuss as a Full Group (10–15 minutes)

- Are there situations in which we need to provide more innovative solutions to our customers? *(List these on the whiteboard.)*

- How can we prepare differently for customer meetings, based on needing to listen differently for their concerns? Does the Trust and Value Ladder image help identify ways?

- As we listen for concerns, are there clarifying questions we need to be asking? Would these answers change the offers you'd make? If so, how?

- Is this going to be easy or difficult to do on a consistent basis? What might get in our way?

- Are there situations in which you, as a customer, need to be more specific in articulating your concerns?

- What are the benefits to us as individuals and as a team by doing this?

Activity 4: Wrap Up and Action Steps

Required time: 10 minutes

Note to Conversation Leaders: This is where you bring it all together for the group and talk about how each person will choose something to work on over the next thirty days, as a first step towards improving how work is managed within the group.

Introduction for the Group

Put the following in your own words:

- The final piece in our conversation is to think about what we intend to do differently based on what we've learned. We'll commit to one change to practice over the next thirty days.

- We focus on supporting each other by making regular check-ins to meet our commitment goals.

Questions for the Group (5–10 minutes)

- What's one thing you plan to implement or do differently over the next thirty days as a result of our conversation today?

- What does success look like to you? How would your organization or industry benefit from this change?

- How can we support each other in achieving our commitments?

Commitments

Participants can choose one of the following commitments or create their own:

- I will use the framework provided here to observe and document my own concerns in the following areas: my life in general, my career, my particular project, my relationship with my boss, my relationship with my peers.

- Before I head to a meeting, I will use the framework provided here to document my assessment of the concerns of the person I am meeting.

- If I want to build trust with another person, I will use the framework provided here to determine how to make effective offers to them. I will make a specific offer that I believe will support their concerns and is something I am committed to doing with excellence.

4

The New View of Projects

or, Getting Real Results

"We will not use our minds and hearts to warehouse facts or pain. We will use them for what they were designed for— for thinking, connecting, listening, and empathizing."
ANONYMOUS

OKAY, WE'VE looked at the principles and individual-level basics of engaging and co-inventing with your work peers; now it's time to level up and see how to scale this with our team and other collaborators. Let's look at how this network of dynamic commitments can be applied to what seems like the most concrete unit of delivery in a workplace and in life: the project. This is where the rubber hits the road.

Projects might seem like the ultimate input-process-output function, a machine designed for the accumulation of a list of completed tasks. But if we reimagine a project as a group effort laden with the potential to spawn innovative thinking, it becomes something that we are striving to produce for our own satisfaction and that of our customers. Human Innovation offers a new way to view projects and the work involved in finalizing them: as an opportunity to practice and execute our new commitment management strategies, apply our enhanced relationship management practices, and hone our new coordination skill set.

Take, for example, that remodel you've been dying to do in your kitchen. That remodel includes a collection of tasks, some of which seem unappealing. However, because you have your vision of the completed project and its full context, you work to communicate that vision to the contractor and subcontractors. Through this process, you know that when you are finished with the project, the kitchen will be beautiful, satisfying, and an overall improvement to your home and—hopefully—quality of life. Throughout the whole project, you are managing commitments with the contractors, and you are talking with them about designs, materials, and results. Anyone who has done a home-improvement project knows that without active co-invention of the conditions of satisfaction, your chances of getting a result that delights you are low.

If you take this practice into a work environment, you and your team will produce something that is bigger than the sum of its parts. The way it gets there is through our practices for co-invention. We have practices for conversations about speculation, design, action, and even for different types of conversations. We also make a practice of managing expectations and having conversations externally with our customer so that we can continue to refine the conditions of satisfaction. Through this engagement, our understanding of what the project can truly deliver develops.

A New Common Sense about Projects

Much has been written about projects, programs, and their management. We have studied, tracked, analyzed, and done postmortems, after-action reviews, and any number of improvement programs and processes since the notion of management of work was first formalized by the French engineer Henri Fayol in the early 1900s. Yet, 65 to 75 percent of all projects still fail.

Recent generations have seen massive social and technological changes, but little has shifted in project management. We still manage our projects as if they are production lines.

The general education level in society has increased significantly, and most people working on projects are now highly paid knowledge workers. Yet, our project management systems and approaches treat them like undereducated production line workers in the 1930s.

In a study of some 250 large software projects between 1995 and 2004—including software systems, information systems, outsource projects, and defense applications—only 10 percent achieved their scheduled cost and quality objectives. Fifty had delays and overruns below 35 percent, while about 175 (70 percent!) experienced major delays and overruns and were terminated without completion.

So, how can project management increase the odds of success?

In the early '90s, I had the privilege of working with Fernando Flores. Flores introduced me to the notion that processes are networks of commitments, an idea he expanded on in his book *Conversations for Action and Collected Essays.* Over the years, I have applied this idea to projects, and I have found that, however we choose to manage our projects, our chances of success are significantly increased when we design them as networks of commitments. Why don't we do it more often? Because—here we go again—it's not common sense.

Let's look at the origin of our current common sense for project management.

In the 1870s, Henri Fayol established the command-and-control model that we currently understand as project management. He proposed that successful management required five basic functions:

1 Forecast and plan the future by preparing plans of action
2 Organize the structure, people, and material
3 Command activity

4 Coordinate, unify, and harmonize effort

5 Control to assure the policies and plans are followed

These functions made good sense when applied to the issues, levels of education, autonomy, and technology of the 1800s. As late as 1940, less than 24 percent of the US population had graduated high school. Today, that number is 90 percent. We are dealing with a fundamentally different working population. Yet our project management common sense has changed little from Fayol's time. Admit it: Fayol's principles look perfectly sensible, don't they? You'd hardly even notice that they treat educated, skilled people as machine parts.

In 1982, Fernando Flores proposed a different definition of management built on the idea of organizations making and keeping commitments. He described management as openness, listening, and eliciting commitments, primarily through promises and requests that allow for the autonomy of a productive unit. In this case, the productive unit is a person. Flores believed that communication between individuals is an invitation to action.

With this (now familiar) thinking, we can reinterpret the basic functions of project management:

- Lead the design of a network of commitments to deliver the desired results

- Recognize that the desired results will emerge and evolve over the course of the project as our understanding becomes more sophisticated

- Engage the network of commitments to define, iterate, and evolve the desired results

- Mobilize people and resources to achieve more than they imagined possible

- Balance the desires of the customer with the time, energy, and capabilities of the team

- Design and negotiate effective mutual commitments to produce satisfaction on the agreed time and investment

The Agile Project Management approach—introduced in 2000 by a team of seventeen software developers including Martin Fowler, Jim Highsmith, Jon Kern, Jeff Sutherland, Ken Schwaber, and Robert C. Martin—captures some of this thinking. It taps into the understanding that humans can accommodate change readily and do not always need to be told what to do.

This is true. Humans are agile. However, projects are not.

We need to design projects from the perspective of the human. We limit ourselves when we design from the perspective of the project. By better designing the project as a network of human commitments, we are putting the human (our most agile actor) at the center of our design, and that builds agility into our projects.

Designing Projects as Networks of Commitments

Most projects start with requirements. But that presupposes the customer is capable of developing a full set of requirements and that the team is trained to co-invent those requirements with the customer. When we start projects by looking at requirements as if they already exist, we are setting ourselves up for failure from the get-go. We are assuming that somebody has a blueprint in their head, and we're falling back into the old command-and-control style of work, believing the leader has all the answers.

Instead, we need to ask ourselves, "What will it take to satisfy the customer?" We need to ask the customer, "What will it take to satisfy you?" We are not asking them for a pre-made blueprint of what the system, solution, innovation, or product should look like; instead, we are guiding them towards a shared and deep understanding of the purpose and value of the project. We engage with them at a fundamentally different level that leads us not to the *thing* but to the *experience* that the customer is looking to have, to their concerns so we can make offers that address them. We build a shared future with them. We are not listening for them to tell us what to do. We are inventing the future with them.

I inherited a team of information technology security experts at one point in my career. When I arrived, the department was struggling with customer satisfaction. There was deep distrust between them and their customers, which were large university research departments. The IT department was staying relatively well on budget, but the value they were providing was in serious dispute. Their internal customers were under a lot of pressure because recently the external customers had significantly increased their security standards for any online collaboration. The IT security team had put together a plan to deal with these new standards: their idea was to implement new software across the entire campus. I believed that this was mostly because their customers didn't understand information security well and were sold on the idea that software could solve their problem.

I took the team to do listening interviews with some senior internal and external customers to understand their concerns and why they thought it was worth spending millions of dollars on software. Through this process, I realized that the idea of asking our customers for requirements was faulty; our team was much better off to listen to them and understand how security would affect them as people. I discovered that they had asked for software only because they thought it was a software problem. But that line of thinking was an important part of why they had a problem in the first place. The number one problem in security is people. If you're in a high-security building, it doesn't matter how reliable the locks are if your staff keep holding the door open for strangers. And according to a study by IBM, human error is the main cause of 95 percent of cyber security breaches.

I came back with an offer to train them to be advocates for their own security as they worked on both our internal and online systems. Our instances of user-created problems related to security dropped significantly. It was also the cheapest solution, and we were able to invest our dollars in protection of our firewall since we were regularly targeted by hackers. Our customers subsequently had fewer systems outages and were significantly less affected by hackers in their day-to-day work.

By listening to our customers, understanding the context and the biggest lever for impact, and having the freedom to make a counteroffer, we shifted their interpretation of information security and improved our own internal customer satisfaction metrics by more than 10 percent.

There are many times when we look to tools—products and software—to solve problems that we believe we understand. Then we bring those tools to customers and try to adapt them to what we believe are their requirements. If, instead, we first listen to the customer's concerns and understand how together we can design conditions of satisfaction (which are sometimes much more simple) to serve their desires for the future, we can deliver much more value and higher customer satisfaction.

Project management can become a practice of moving from inert task lists to promises to real people; from project plans with tasks and subtasks to project plans that track commitments and customers and performers.

From Commands to Commitments

From	To
Commands	Commitments
Input-process-output	Networks of commitment
Task lists	Promises to people
Waterfall	Tracking commitments
Plans to finish the project	Project plans to satisfy the customer
Getting it done	Building value

Designing, creating, and managing networks of commitments is also driven by the Three Engines of Capacity Development, which I introduced in chapter 1 and will cover in depth in chapter 6. As you get good at managing your own commitments, you can extend that observation capacity and experience to your team members and ultimately to your full network of commitments—the ecosystem in which you work. By doing this, you create reinforcing practices of Observe-Experience-Amplify and establish an engine for capacity and mindset development.

Real Project Results Using Commitment-Based Management

For inspiration (and for all you lovely skeptics), here's an example of the value we have created through managing projects as networks of commitments. Our project was to apply human-centered process design to improve efficiency and increase available sales time. We achieved a 10 percent increase over a three-month period as a result of specific process cycle time reductions; following our initial project, this group was expanded to include in excess of $1 billion in additional portfolio. We implemented customer-centered processes and commitment-based partnerships to improve customer satisfaction and reduce service cycle time. It realized a 13 percent increase in customer satisfaction in a three-month period; previous increases averaged only 1 percent per month. And the company's own service-support group survey showed increases in responsiveness averaging 4 percent and an improvement in quality of service averaging 10 percent, and the department was ranked "most improved" in an internal quality survey.

We introduced a new way of thinking about information processes to integrate people, process, and technology and to deliver a step change in IT service center customer satisfaction, and we saw these results:

- Within the space of two months, 14,000 backlogged cases were eliminated.

- Fifty percent of cases were now resolved and closed the same day.

- Voicemail volume was reduced by 55 percent as customers called back less frequently.

- The chances of speaking to an account representative went from 1 in 10 to 1 in 4.

I did this by working with the support team to show them how to make real commitments, how to negotiate effective promises with their customers, and how to design standards that were doable. The standards were what they could realistically deliver on, and they no longer sold hope to their customer only to ultimately disappoint them. The team members quickly understood that customers prefer to be treated like adults and with respect. Customers were, in fact, much more appreciative of the service center team negotiating and making real commitments, managing and delivering on them, than being sold a load of hope.

Once you start managing projects as networks of commitments, you take advantage of the huge lever that is trust. We do many things to try to build trust within teams—offsites, away days, retreats, all kinds of team building—yet we miss the opportunity to build trust in a systematic, day-to-day way by simply designing, developing, delivering, and declaring satisfaction on the everyday requests, offers, and promises we make to each other. We navigate several hundred commitments a day, thousands a year—and millions among a team. By managing our projects as networks of commitments, we create an environment and systems that align with who we are: human beings seeking to build trust with and deliver value to each other.

In order to better understand networks of commitments inside our work structures, we can apply these practices to projects, which offer us a fertile training ground. Every project comes with a variety of commitments that need to be completed to move forward. Each commitment is likely related to a person or an objective. When we carry out these project commitments in alignment with the interpersonal and horizontal commitments we're developing inside our work environment, we can expand our capacity for successful execution.

My team and I were working for a large network equipment manufacturer that had been working to get a product out the door for six years. Despite the best efforts of the design, engineering, manufacturing, marketing, and sales teams, they were failing miserably. And they knew it and suffered with it. We brought the leaders of those teams together, took their existing project plan, and asked them to identify who was the customer and the performer for each task. That helped them discover hundreds of tasks in the project plan that were unconnected to major requests that the team leaders were making each other in this highly cross-functional environment.

Then we put aside the project plan, and we discussed who was making requests to whom and identified the major commitments needed. Every single one of these smart, capable, intelligent people knew what needed to happen for the product to get out the door. They just didn't have the practices to orchestrate that process for themselves. Through a series of conversations over two to three days, the highly complicated project and task management environment became a high-level and complex but navigable series of commitments that each leader was ready to make. From there, we looked at how to execute within each functional area. Rather than list out a number of tasks in each functional area, each area head made requests to their people by name, and we were able to rationalize and consolidate the project plan from ten thousand tasks to an initial 126 requests and commitments at the leadership level. Within each functional group, there were about five hundred commitments to be made. This simplification, rationalization, and contextualization of interpersonal (customer and performer) and horizontal, cross-functional commitments allowed this team to successfully deliver a product to market within six months, and that product continued to deliver revenue for the company for a decade.

Large projects have a historically high rate of failure. Our long-standing de facto approach deserves an update. Instead of managing a project as if it's a laundry list of tasks, reconceptualizing the project as the final result of networked collaboration provides more opportunity for workplace cooperation and mutual investment.

Dynamic Shared Commitments

Dynamic shared commitments are the foundation of successful projects. The Co-inventing Dynamic Deliverables diagram looks at the relationship between malicious compliance and co-invention, between static coerced tasks and dynamic shared commitments. I also distinguish between static deliverables and dynamic deliverables. Static deliverables are discrete, preidentified tasks that are usually highly repetitive.

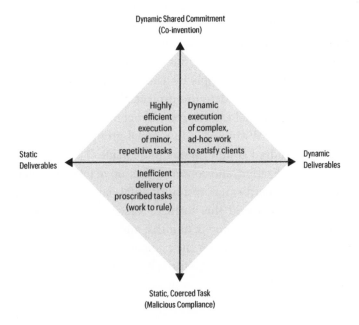

Co-Inventing Dynamic Deliverables

Dynamic Shared Commitment
(Co-invention)

Static Deliverables

Dynamic Deliverables

Highly efficient execution of minor, repetitive tasks

Dynamic execution of complex, ad-hoc work to satisfy clients

Inefficient delivery of proscribed tasks (work to rule)

Static, Coerced Task
(Malicious Compliance)

We talked in chapter 3 about malicious compliance in a situation where static deliverables and tasks are allocated and tracked, without any co-invention or negotiation by the individuals involved. This generally results in inefficient delivery of prescribed tasks—in other words, work to rule. Obviously, this is an ineffective way to create innovation capacity.

Static deliverables delivered with dynamic, shared commitments look more like the management of a procedure than that of a process or network of commitments. For example, a project needs to happen in the event of a cyber security attack: each team has a very specific list of things, ideally a checklist, which they know they need to do; these are repetitive tasks executed on an ongoing basis. However, successful defense from the cyberattack is dependent on the co-invention that happens in the moment among the team. That drives the decision-making and is dependent on the shared interpretation of the data coming from the repetitive tasks. Any kind of emergency response has elements that fit into this category.

Dynamic shared commitments and dynamic deliverables are the trickiest types of networks of commitments to successfully manage—because they cannot really be managed. They require each person in the network of commitment to manage themselves (autonomy). And they require the person guiding and leading the work to be masterful at orchestrating dynamic networks of commitment. In an innovation or research project environment, for example, you are not really managing a project: you are holding space for innovation to emerge. Sometimes you are holding up a mirror to the team so they can see where they are, where they're headed, and how orchestrated they are. But you are not assigning tasks, as one does in a traditional project management approach.

The fourth quadrant is intentionally left blank—there is no way to achieve dynamic deliverables with static, coerced tasks or malicious compliance.

As you set up programs and projects, it helps to be honest about the type of project you are leading and to develop your project management approach accordingly. This will set you up to hone your ability to manage dynamic shared commitments. It's also very useful to know when you have a mix of types within one project—you could have static and dynamic deliverables within the same project. Getting smart about your checklists of static deliverables frees up more time to do the co-invention work for the dynamic deliverables.

Design Itself Can Be Innovative

When we design projects, we may feel pulled between doing exactly what has been done before and starting over from scratch. Most of us have encountered a workplace process that feels rigid and limiting. We are handed a string of directions, as if we are doing a lab experiment in Biology 101, and inevitably we find the directions inflexible and sometimes ill-suited to the project at hand. We naturally want to reconceptualize it. But we can fall into the opposite trap of approaching each new project, each new offer, and each new commitment as if it was our first encounter with the process. In innovative spaces, the tendency to rethink and redesign the process can bog us down.

If we structure our work commitments around fine-tuning the relationships on which they hinge, less of this total overhaul is necessary. Instead of throwing away the process document and starting from scratch with a new process for every project, we can find a new balance. This might look like discussing how our last commitment went. It might look like asking what part of your previous offer landed and what didn't. This places you and your customer, your coworker, back in a design mindset without returning to the drawing board or a blank slate.

Some areas for revision or adjustment might be:

- Quality control standards
- Internal and external standard differentiation
- Review process
- Qualitative measurement

The idea of taking these commitments to expand their application might sound counterintuitive. It is difficult to imagine that a set of shared expectations developed inside one work relationship might translate to another work relationship, or even a similar project. However, the more adept we become at making offers, fine-tuning the delivery process, and managing a set of shared expectations, the more we recognize repetition. Often, conditions of satisfaction are not unique. This is what makes us qualified to do a new job if we leave an old one at a similar level. Sure, there is a period of integration, but the expectations are not entirely alien to us. This is equally true inside networks of commitments. This kind of repetition can once again facilitate agility. Instead of designing a new process for each new project, we can design for a predictable yet nuanced set of shared concerns and expectations. From here, we can streamline.

The ability to do this hinges on understanding conditions of satisfaction and setting standards.

Standards Matter

I've already introduced malicious compliance—and those heaps of black plastic trash bags on London street corners under Maggie Thatcher. That demonstrated some of the things that most undermine our ability to co-invent with other human beings: cynicism, victimization, and blame. When we engage in malicious compliance, it's never because we are jerks who want to irritate everyone around us. We become cynical, feel victimized, or fall into blame because we don't see any alternative. We're groping around with the lights out in a room full of obstacles. One of the biggest levers to move people out of cynicism, victimization, and blame is to talk about standards. It's like turning on the lights: people can see where the obstacles are. It reengages our ability to co-invent.

I'll explain. I went to school for almost twenty years. My teachers had standards, and sometimes they told us what they were. More often, teachers were vaguely dissatisfied with completed assignments. Students had no idea how to course correct for their dissatisfaction. Because we didn't believe that we were allowed to discuss standards, we couldn't imagine co-inventing them. I remember it was only at postgraduate school that we were allowed to have those conversations. That was when we finally had some idea of, and input into, the conditions for satisfaction.

Standards allow us to assess whether or not we're satisfied—and to anticipate whether our customers will be. Good standards that are discussed and understood are then mutually agreed on by the customer and the performer. Sometimes you can take an existing standard and have a conversation about it with a performer, modifying it for your particular circumstances. But it's crucial to bring the topic of standards into the game. It is explicit, not assumed. It's not uninspected common sense. Standards are stated in measurable terms that can be supported by facts.

We tend to park standards outside our purview and responsibility. By not acknowledging, understanding, and leveraging standards, we lose a mechanism for co-invention. When we lack practices for observing or declaring standards, we tend to inherit them from others. For instance, if we don't stop and look at our standards for clothing and appearance, we just follow the standards set by the fashion industry, and the result is clothes that don't look good on most of us and a lot of people who think their bodies are the wrong shape.

Uninspected standards are an even bigger problem if people come into a project with conflicting uninspected standards, and they can't understand why others aren't following common sense. To continue with the clothing example, a company that specializes in technical apparel, say rain jackets made from Gore-Tex, likely requires a different set of standards than a more conventional clothing company. Technical materials must be tested and proven to be functional, apart from the considerations of style. Conflicting and uninspected standards could present a real problem inside a niche industry area, where some industry rules apply but not all—particularly when highly technical output is involved.

If we lack shared standards and have differing expectations, then we set up the cycle of dissatisfaction, resentment, blame, and distrust. Open conversations about standards are the first step forward from this. I'm sure you can remember environments where, because of the resentment, blame, and distrust, these conversations were not had, and the cycle of cynicism, victimization, and blame spiraled.

Co-inventing Standards

Too rarely do we spend time understanding our own standards and proactively communicating them to the people with whom we collaborate. Sometimes even when we do invite people to co-invent, we expect them to read our minds when it comes to standards. But without clear design and co-invention of standards, you're stumbling in the dark. Someone once said to me, "How have you managed to get so much done?" And I said, "Well, what I do is I hire fantastic people, agree on the standards for great work, and then I get the hell out of their way!" That has been my M.O. for most of my career. I'm very aware of standards and co-invent them with people, rather than assume they already know them or dictate mine to them.

Traditionally, we've relied on an imitation of others' standards, and the general standard is usually set by the output of other people. Ideally, a standard becomes the new way of thinking about things, a declaration of value that allows us to assess effectiveness and our own satisfaction. Often I know what I'm looking for but I won't necessarily have a standard; in that case, I talk to an expert who translates my expectation into their standards, which results in a set of shared standards for our goals. This moves away from "I'm copying something that's already been done" to "I have a sense of what is going to produce satisfaction for me" and "How does that translate into your domain of expertise?" It is through a deep acknowledgment of each other's domains of expertise that we have a sense of autonomy and manage our commitments—which precludes the cynicism, victimization, and blame that leads to malicious compliance.

Built into this entire methodology is a push for people to have conversations that they might otherwise avoid or not think to have.

Ineffective standards are those that make it entirely subjective for me to tell you whether or not I like what it is that you're doing. It could be predicated on how I'm feeling: I don't like the color of your shirt, or I'm pissed off with you today.

What we're trying to do is move standards out of this highly subjective environment into something that we've invented together. That oftentimes pushes the envelope, and we do something bigger or better than we ever thought we could.

When I first became a mom, I would give my daughter a punishment and say, "Hey, you shouldn't have done this. Here's how to learn how not to do that again." Until I realized I wasn't practicing what I preached. So, I switched tactics. I would say, "Hey, you did something really foolish. How would you like to not do it again? And how will you know if you've done it again?" She could invent her own learning from this process—which she did. Her standards for her own behavior were higher than my standards for her behavior. But the beauty of this discrepancy was that it got us to have conversations like, "Hey, what are your standards for how to behave? You are who you are; you are going to behave like a decent human being." Designing effective standards together was an essential process of co-invention. Likewise, with teams that I've led, we have these conversations explicitly as a team. We can't quantify everything, but it pushes us towards design conversations.

Declaring Standards

Just as lacking shared standards can lead to the dissatisfaction and cynicism cycle, the corollary is also true: establishing shared standards can support and even produce ambition, confidence, and acceptance. So, how do we declare standards? How do we work them out, set them down, discuss them, and negotiate them?

We're busy. Busier than ever before. As the way we work continues to evolve—requiring more speed, autonomy, and transparency—we need to adapt how we work together. While we have always had high standards for work performance (individually and collectively), these standards were largely established *for* us. Company policies, performance management guidelines, project templates—lots of static documents exist to frame work expectations for us. Now, as the pace of work is changing all aspects of how we work, we need a new approach for agreeing to standards as they evolve. Policies and standards can become outdated the moment they're published; workers need to take ownership for setting standards as the work unfolds, or they risk perpetuating lower standards, which results in frustrated and dissatisfied customers.

Without co-invention of agreed standards, we're left with the risk of an unhappy and blaming customer and a frustrated performer who lacks control. Co-inventing standards turns expectation setting on its head, asking that both parties be vocal in defining the standards of work up front, leading to shared agreement for the quality of outcomes. There are two key insights on this I'd like to share with you.

Declaring Shared Standards Keeps Work Flowing

Given the pace of work today, combined with the high volume of emails, messages, and information coming at us, it's easy to skip the step of pausing to clarify standards. But it's this fast pace that makes clarity even more critical. By clarifying what good looks like (as expectations from the requester, and standards from the performer), we prevent rework later.

A long, formal process isn't required—we don't need a six-level signature sequence—but if you declare the quality level as you confirm the work content and deadlines, the work keeps moving forward. This also entails touching base as needed, as new criteria or situations emerge, or agreeing to check in on an established frequency (e.g., weekly) to create an opportunity for either party to surface issues that may impact expectations.

Being Crystal Clear Saves Time

At the speed most teams are working, it's easy to miss nuanced language when expectations are conveyed in vague terms. You need to be clear in sharing specific standards you intend to meet. Ask for greater clarity when others make or agree to standards.

Clear standards:

- Allow us to ground an assessment of satisfaction or dissatisfaction
- Are mutually agreed upon by the customer and performer
- Are explicit (i.e., not assumed)
- Are stated in measurable terms
- Can be supported by facts

Instead of Saying	Say
"I'll aim for today."	"I'll send the revisions by 5 p.m."
"We set high standards."	"90 percent of customers will rate us at least 4 out of 5."
"We hope people like working here."	"We work to maintain less than 5 percent voluntary turnover."
"I'll try to get back to you about that."	"I'll send an initial draft of the document that answers all of the questions you've asked."

Declaring standards and mechanisms for revising standards in a shared, coordinated way takes work but ultimately saves time and frustration. It leads to greater productivity and an environment that is more conducive to innovation.

Standards and Metrics

We might be able to see what we can impact—for example, we have a strong sense that a gender-balanced customer-facing team might increase customer satisfaction, particularly in the consumer goods market—but we will have no understanding of the magnitude of the impact without standards to measure it. We can't show the value of the impact without measuring it. That may seem to go without saying, but I have come across many change programs that have no real business metrics. I find the following little statement useful:

Declare Standards + Measure Goals + Maintain Progress = Show Value

Here we can begin to see the relationship between standards, goals, and progress. Since our purpose is to show value around what matters to our customer, you can see how important it is to understand the standards by which we are measured, the goals we establish with our customers, and the progress we report to continue to build trust.

Standards can also show us how to make our desired impact. The Standards and Impact table will help you understand the importance and potential impact of exactly who the customer is for the metric and who the customer is for the standard.

Standards and Impact

	Internal Customer	External Customer
Internal Metric	Operational improvement	Customer satisfaction
External Metric	Move the needle	Strategic impact

Oftentimes it is easy for teams or organizations to hide behind their metrics. You can do this if you have an internal metric with an internal customer. This can, of course, lead to operational improvement, but you need to be clear about how this will impact the external customer.

An external metric with an internal customer, on the other hand, would be something like market share. An improvement in market share tells us that we are gaining market share, which is great. But it doesn't tell us why.

Standards that involve an internal metric with an external customer are usually designed to address customer satisfaction or shareholder value. But these only work well if we really understand what it takes to satisfy the customer. For example, if we want to impact customer satisfaction, which has historically been low, and 85 percent of the people phoning the car company call center are women, then we might determine that by putting more women on the front lines of our call center we can improve customer satisfaction. We won't know until we test it, so by understanding what satisfaction means to our customers (e.g., Are they listened to or talked down to? Are they dealt with promptly?), we increase our chances of calibrating correctly until we get the desired impact. We are essentially co-inventing this standard with our customers. The closer we get to them and the better we listen and engage with them, the stronger the co-invention. And this does not only apply to B2C environments.

Ultimately, when you measure value to your external customers, you need to do so via an external third party—for example, industry awards with hard metrics behind them, best in call awards, or consumer satisfaction awards.

The bottom line is don't hide behind your metrics. As much as you can, get out there with your customers and design shared standards for creating satisfaction. It will make you more innovative in the long run. And it's a great way to dynamically listen to customers while designing together with structure and purpose, something you will never get from just interviewing.

Breakdowns Happen

Okay, so you're beginning to move into this new way of common sense, this new way of thinking about work, and you start practicing this conversational loop, and then…life happens. Breakdowns happen. Things don't go according to plan. So, what do you do? How do you deal with it? How do you think about it? How do you reframe it, and how do you move forward?

1. Recognize That There Is a Breakdown

Step one is recognizing a breakdown. This is, as you'll remember, the most basic level of concern to listen for. It's like when your car breaks down: you're moving forward, everything is going fine, and all of a sudden, your tire blows out, or you have problems with your engine, or you run out of gas. This happens in life—and in projects—a lot. We can anticipate it and we can plan for it, but inevitably it happens.

Pretending it hasn't happened is like driving on a flat tire or with a busted axle or no brakes.

Why would we pretend a breakdown hasn't happened? Because we've been taught since we were very small to believe that breakdowns are bad. I forget my homework; I get into trouble. I speak too much in class; I get reprimanded. I break a dish; I get screamed at—or I scream at myself. We have it burned into our consciousness that we should be sufficiently in control of things that breakdowns don't happen. But stuff happens with no intentionality on our part. That's the way life goes.

This old common sense tends to make us very nervous when breakdowns happen, and we're hesitant to even talk about them. And if we actually say hey, this is broken, this didn't work, I broke this, and I apologize, people often feel uncomfortable, underappreciated, or blamed. We are so conditioned to believe that breakdowns are bad that when you first declare a breakdown, if the person you declare it to is junior to you, they will likely hear, "It's your fault that you didn't make this happen, and I can't believe that you did this." They will feel that you think they did it on purpose, that they're ineffective or stupid or malicious. If they're feeling unjustly impugned, they may think, "I'll get even with you eventually." This is obviously not a super effective way of engaging with people or of reducing the overall number of problems you have. So you become hesitant to have those conversations. Many times, we view these conversations as confrontational. We have to gear ourselves up to have these conversations, to walk into someone's office and make this huge fuss about something that says you shouldn't have done it this this way. Even if you didn't cause the breakdown, in certain cultures, the messenger gets shot. In some organizations, the people who declare a breakdown get fired or demoted.

If, instead, we reframe breakdowns and think about them in a different way, we free ourselves up to take a different kind of action. We need to remind ourselves, and reaffirm to others, that breakdowns are not just inevitable—which they are, like gravity and time—but are opportunities to understand how things work, what their weak points are, and how to design them better.

2. Declare the Breakdown

Step two is to declare the breakdown. Declaring breakdowns is a valuable and essential process for a responsible person working in an organization. And it is not easy to do. It's also an important part of upholding shared standards. If you are committed to success, excellence, and mastery in your work, then declaring breakdowns is an essential practice.

Declaring a breakdown is not about blaming someone. Declaring a breakdown is about acknowledging that something didn't go according to plan and requesting that we move forward to execute the plan more effectively and not have the breakdown happen again.

The most effective way to get the ball rolling on declaring breakdowns is to do it yourself. After all, as the messenger and the leader, you are ultimately responsible, and you won't shoot yourself, it's not effective to blame yourself, and you know it's not effective to blame your team members. Since you are committed to developing this practice, you can sweat your way through the discomfort.

The conversation can be as simple as: you recognize a breakdown (your boss may be yelling at you), you pull your team together, and say, "Hey, I think we have a breakdown." You state the breakdown and say, "I'd like to brainstorm with you to see if it's lack of shared standards, unclear conditions of satisfaction, fumbled negotiation, if I dropped the ball or one of us did, or if there's lack of clarity around who the customer is for the work. Let's pull it apart and see how to resolve this immediate breakdown and improve our coordination, so we avoid breakdowns like this as much as possible in the future."

Your vibe is that breakdowns happen, you assume everyone was doing their best, and the goal is not to assign blame but to fix it, learn from it, and coordinate better together going forward. Try it out—if you don't bring a whiff of blame into the room, it pretty much works like a charm every time.

3. Co-Invent a Novel Approach

Next, we find ourselves discussing what happened so we can move forward in the right way. Most of us have had the experience of repair inside a friendship or romantic relationship. Sometimes we see this in a work relationship as well. One party involved in the breakdown or conflict makes some kind of effort to ease the tension: they laugh, they joke, they somehow acknowledge their own silliness in the face of strife. From there, we begin to design something different. We've broken the tension, now we're on even footing, and we can strategize safely together as cocreators. This requires both of us to take a second look at the problem with fresh eyes.

Underlying this willingness to declare and discuss breakdowns is a different way of looking at accountability. When you establish a baseline acceptance that breakdowns happen, and approach each one with an attitude of "Hey, we made a mistake, let's talk about it and see how we can fix it or do it better next time," you're sharing responsibility, and you're asking them to work with you to resolve the issue. What they'll hear is "I respect you enough to hold you to the standards that you and I have agreed to, and I want to continue to build trust with you." You learn how to calibrate and recalibrate with each other much, much more effectively.

The details vary, naturally. The approach is different depending on who you're talking to. I've been doing this work for so long now that sometimes when I recognize that a breakdown has happened, I'll take a step back and think, "Do I actually want to go to the trouble of working with this person to help them learn how to avoid this in the future?" or, for instance, with a contractor for a limited job such as a repair. "Am I fine to just step away, find another provider to do the work for me, and move on?" When we're asking people to accept a new level of responsibility, we're making a commitment to them at the same time. We're offering to help them do this learning to recalibrate with us and move to the next level of competence in engaging with us. Which means we need to be able to handle that commitment.

4. Everyone Can Declare Breakdowns

You can't be the only person declaring breakdowns. Anyone who sees one needs to be able to declare one—to put their hand up and say, "I think we have a breakdown happening here," "I don't think this project is going to get delivered on time," or "I don't think this innovation is valuable." This doesn't always happen. As mentioned, the vast majority of product launches fail, and less "than 3 percent of new consumer packaged goods exceed first-year sales of $50 million." Somewhere in the process for each of those products, somebody could have said "I don't think this is quite going to work," but either they weren't listened to or they didn't feel safe to say so—because they didn't want to get the blame.

When you are engaging your team and stuff goes wrong, if you can discipline yourself to say, "I understand people make mistakes; the question is, How do we design our way out of this together?" then you're doing a couple of things. One, you're inviting your team to learn with you. You're acknowledging that breakdowns happen and that people don't necessarily have to shoulder the blame for them. You're asking them to take responsibility—to *share* responsibility—and you're opening the door for a conversation for design that assumes best intentions.

One of the companies I work for right now has the value of "assume best intent." When we assume best intent, we invite people to co-invent with us, to design with us, to learn with us, and we move ourselves out of a blame and retribution environment. We keep the channels open to talk to each other. Innovation happens from human beings talking to each other. If we deeply believe that innovation happens through human beings coordinating and creating a future together, then we need to get excellent at this process of execution to open up the door for building trust and partnerships.

Key Practice: Developing and Managing Networks of Commitments

This key practice is a set of group activities. You can't learn to observe and orchestrate networks of commitments alone. They're taken from my Next Level Innovations Leaders program; one of the practices we focus on is helping leaders observe and mobilize networks of commitments.

Conversation Timeline
- Activity 1: What Is Work Anyway?: 10 minutes
- Activity 2: Making Work Work for You: 15 minutes
- Activity 3: Identifying Real Conversations that Need to Be Had: 25 minutes
- Activity 4: Wrap Up and Action Steps: 10 minutes

Activity 1: What Is Work Anyway?
Required time: 10 minutes

Required supplies: Whiteboard and markers

Note to Conversation Leaders: This conversation is about understanding the relationships between promises and execution and innovation. If we want to have flexibility and agency inside our organizations, we need to accept responsibility for the promises we make. This will be hard for some people who are uncomfortable with making explicit promises. The purpose here is to ask people to park their reservations and simply practice. Some people will struggle with the accountability of making real promises, but the upside is people will trust and like you more, and work in general is more enjoyable.

Prep Work

Each person should come to the conversation having watched the YouTube video "Promise Based Management: Execution Part 1."

Introduction for the Group

Put the following in your own words:

- Companies spend a lot of time and resources trying to figure out how to improve cross-functional collaboration. Google's Project Oxygen, which is designed to understand what makes a great manager and leader, identifies "collaborates cross-functionally" as a key capability.

- What many companies fail to recognize is that collaboration and cross-functional collaboration happen when people make promises to each other.

- In the video, Donald Sull, a professor from the London Business School, identifies three ways of "getting things done": power, procedure (which he refers to as *process*; we distinguish between process and procedure), and promise.

- Promise-Based Management is the most effective way to get things done when dealing with smart, educated people interested in innovation, agility, flexibility, and their own agency.

- However, we have not been trained to see requests, offers, and promises, so we need to train ourselves to see and learn how to use them as a common language to get work done efficiently and with more trust, enjoyment, and creativity.

- This module is designed to help your team see requests, offers, and promises and to apply those practices to getting things done within the team, where you are all practicing together, and eventually with other teams cross-functionally.

Questions for the Group (3–5 minutes)

- What resonated most for you in the video?

- What caught your attention? Why?

- What do you think your role is in a "dynamic network of commitments"?

Note to Conversation Leaders: You may want to draw this model on the whiteboard.

Depths of Listening

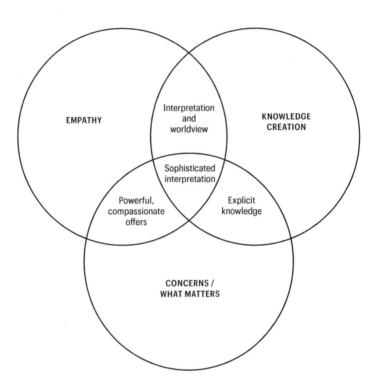

Wrap Up (1–2 minutes)

Put the following in your own words:

- Most of the world views work as a set of tasks that must be done to produce a product. This made sense when our work was primarily in manufacturing, when very few people had any education and they needed to be told what to do.

- When we work in highly complex environments, this no longer makes sense. Excellence in complex environments requires the brilliance of everyone involved. No one person has all the answers; no one person can hold the vision alone; no one person has a blueprint for where we are going or what we are doing.

- Work needs to move from being the completion of a set of predefined tasks to a dynamic network of commitments made by observant, conscious, highly skilled, and knowledgeable human beings who are agents in creating their own futures and the future of the companies in which they choose to work.

- By learning to have conversations for getting things done, we can transform the way we and our organizations work and innovate.

Activity 2: Making Work Work for You

Required time: 15 minutes

Note to Conversation Leaders: It is important, if somewhat uncomfortable, to help people see what is not working and how they, as individuals, have the power to change it. Try to be comfortable exploring the pain, knowing that it will get better by the end of this module when people are given the tools to fix what is not working.

Introduction for the Group

Put the following in your own words:

- Many people live in overwhelm at work. Most of us spend our days coping rather than creating. Yet we deeply desire to create. If we spend our days coping instead of creating, we live our lives in drudgery.

- The key to changing this is to engage with each other in the act of creating promises that we make to each other.

- This activity is designed to help you see how work is really a dynamic network of promises made to each other.

- It is important to know that there are no right or wrong answers for this activity; what matters here is that you identify how you make requests and promises, how others make request and promises, and how that impacts their ability to work with you and your ability to work with them.

- This is an opportunity not to judge others but to work on changing how you make requests and promises and to see how that can change how you work with others and how it can positively impact your enjoyment of work.

Questions to Discuss in Smaller Groups (7–10 minutes)

Think through your answers to these questions on your own for a minute before discussing in pairs (or groups of three):

- How much time is wasted working on unclear requests?

- How many promises do you have floating out there with customers hoping that they are going to happen and yet you only vaguely remember them?

- If you were able to clear up even just your own part of the mess, would this make life and work better? More enjoyable? Less stressful?

Questions to Discuss as a Group (5–7 mins)

Uncommitted customers lob incomplete requests over the wall (or partition) and are not committed to helping you help them be satisfied.

- What did your pair or group of three see about the negative impact of unclear requests and uncommitted customers?

- How would our work environment be better if we committed to make complete requests and real promises to each other?

Activity 3: Identifying Real Conversations That Need to Be Had

Required time: 25 minutes
Required supplies: Pen, paper, whiteboard, and markers

Introduction for the Group
Put the following in your own words:

- This is where we put it into action what we've learned with each other and with our team leaders.

- We all understand that it will be a little awkward at first; we won't get it right the first time, and we will be clumsy and we may irritate each other.

- Knowing that, let's commit to help each other and give each other space and time to collectively get better at this, believing that it will support our enjoyment of working together and help us to be more efficient and innovative.

Individual Reflection (3–5 minutes)

- Think about two or three requests that you have made.

- Who have you made them to? Write down the person's name.

- Do you think that you are both on the same page?

- Are you clear on what you have been asked to do?

- If it is a request, do you feel that the other person is clear on what they have been asked to do? Do they feel like you have their back and are there to help them or answer any questions? Or have you lobbed your request over the wall and run off?

Questions to Discuss in Pairs or Groups of Three (5–10 minutes)

Invite participants to be curious and listen actively as their partners share their thoughts and experiences. Remind everyone that this is not an opportunity to moan about the lobbers but is an opportunity to identify with real human beings you need to talk to.

- Take the requests and/or promises that you have identified from the work above and discuss them with your partner.

- What is the best way to approach the request or promise?

- Are there similar issues or conversations that need to be had?

- Are you ready to commit to having this conversation in the next day or two?

- Take turns practicing these conversations.

- Be prepared to talk about what you have noticed.

Questions to Discuss as a Full Group (10 minutes)

- What have you realized as a result of these activities?

- How common is it to be carrying around a "stress bag" of incomplete requests and promises?

- How does this get in the way of having fun working together? Doing productive work together? Innovating and bringing our most brilliant selves to work?

Activity 4: Wrap Up and Action Steps

Required time: 10 minutes

Introduction for the Group

Put the following in your own words:

- The final piece in our conversation is to discuss what we intend to do differently based on what we've learned. We'll commit to one change to practice over the next thirty days.

- It's important to think about how these changes can benefit us as individuals and as a team.

Questions for the Group (5–10 minutes)

- What's one thing you plan to implement or do differently over the next thirty days as a result of our conversations today?

- What does success look like for our group?

- How can we support each other in achieving this commitment?

Commitments

The following commitments are samples to choose from, or they can make their own commitment.

- I am going to pay attention to how I and others make requests, which requests are complete and efficient, and which are not.

- When I am unclear or sense that I am not on the same page as my customer, I will ask for clarification.

- I am going to be honest with myself and with others about what I can promise to do and what I cannot. A decline is also a promise.

5

Empathy and Mastery

or, Inventing the Future Together

"*My imagination makes me human and makes me a fool;
it gives me all the world and exiles me from it.*"

URSULA K. LE GUIN

GOOD WORK with the right people makes you happy. We know that instinctively, but there's even scientific proof for it. Experiments show that having a sense of higher purpose stimulates oxytocin production, and so does trust. Trust and purpose then reinforce each other, providing a mechanism for extended oxytocin release, which produces happiness. So, joy on the job comes from doing purpose-driven work with a trusted team.

As we saw in chapter 4, projects are networks of commitments. That means that trust is at the heart of a successful project. Trust allows us room to grow, play, and expand and also to negotiate and renegotiate. Developing conditions of satisfaction, inside or outside a project, requires trust. After conditions of satisfaction, empathy comes as the foundation for design, and it supports us in our pursuit of mastery and appreciation of the evolving mastery of others.

Trust is also relevant outside projects. As we move away from the exclusively top-down management strategies that have dominated the workplace until now, designing trust relationships can help us leverage networks of commitment. A highly developed and fluid network of commitments—coupled with a nuanced understanding of how to design and carry out agreements, make offers, and deliver on those offers—encourages trust relationships, and it lays a foundation for co-invention. For us to co-invent agile, committed networks, we need to systematically build trust all the time in our work environments. If I make a verbal accord with someone on my team, and we take the time to seriously discuss the conditions of satisfaction for this verbal agreement, we need a shared belief that all involved actors are trustworthy. Shared standards allow us to ground that assessment of satisfaction or dissatisfaction.

Trust and shared standards also function best when there is a lateral, mutual commitment. While a top-down management strategy requires a lot of energetic output and demands that a supervisor monitor, assemble, and oversee every involved step, a lateral commitment built on mutual interest and trust allows for a more hands-off approach.

Imagine you're a parent whose child is struggling with their math homework. You see that they're struggling, and instead of working through the problems with them, you do all their math homework yourself. This doesn't solve the problem—it makes a bigger problem! Twice the amount of effort and energy is expended: the kid expends effort and energy struggling to complete the math problems, and then you, the parent, actually do all of the work. In the long run, you have also made more work for yourself: you've kept your kid from learning, thereby ensuring you will have to provide the answers again on a subsequent problem set. If, instead, you trust your kid to finish their math homework and understand that the objective of homework is not only to get as many correct answers as possible but also to understand how to tackle the problem set at hand, you can work with them to get better results and save work later. Likewise, at work, the team members who understand that their coworkers are committed to the same outcomes as they are, and who communicate in order to arrive at a mutually agreeable output, leverage trust to get the work done well.

Making Offers Builds Trust

Making carefully designed, unsolicited, intentional offers to our coworkers and team members is another way of building trust internally. When we demonstrate a nuanced understanding of all the moving parts in a deliverable, and those related to a specific outcome, we at once increase our own agility and inspire trust in us from others. Our coworkers can come to rely on us to understand what they are asking for. Better yet, they can hope we might understand what they have yet to ask for.

Aiming for this kind of intentional offering also encourages others to trust us with a variety of responsibilities and allows us to better curate what kind of work we spend our time doing. Zeroing in on something we want to offer our team means spending time on what we want and becoming attuned to what kind of offers make sense to deliver inside our commitment networks.

A colleague of mine once told me that you can only make offers as big as the level of trust you have developed. This is particularly important for those of us who get frustrated with the lack of change within our organization. Many times, we can see what needs to be done but we don't have the level of trust to make offers big enough to produce the change we know needs to happen. In circumstances like this, we need to systematically build higher levels of trust to reach greater levels of partnership.

Leveraging the work done by John Searle, Flores, and others in defining offers, promises, and levels of concern, the Trust and Value Ladder (which we first saw in chapter 3) brings together two things that we have already discussed. One is the level of concerns that our customers might have— what matters to them. The other is the types of intentional action we can take based on the trust we have in order to build greater trust and more value. The Trust and Value Ladder will help you see the relationship between listening for what matters to others and anticipating requests and making innovative offers. The more effective your listening, and the more innovative and aligned your offers, the more trust you will build and the more you will be invited to make valuable, impactful offers.

The Trust and Value Ladder

Build Trust and Value		
If you have the courage to	You will	You will be
Make innovative offers	Co-invent to satisfy unexpressed intentions	Trusted and invaluable
Make offers	Satisfy declared intentions	In partnership
Anticipate requests	Make useful promises	Appreciated
Destroy Trust		
Only respond to requests	Create breakdowns	Outsourceable

At the bottom is the level of breakdowns and basic reactions to requests. At this level, we are replaceable, and the work is outsourceable. But as we build trust, we can anticipate requests to help others fulfill their promises. With ever increasing levels of trust, we can make offers to the declared intentions of our teammates and our customers and develop a partnership with them. Over time, we develop a level of co-invention capability with our teammates or our customers, and we begin to have conversations around unexpressed intentions. Together we uncover what really matters to them, and we get invited into a space of creating innovative offers based on deep desires and long-held visions that we can help others realize.

These deep desires and long-held visions are usually in alignment with our own desires and passions, and that gives us an opportunity to really share the concerns of our customers and teammates and create something greater than either of us could have done individually. This is true partnership based on a deep practice of building, maintaining, and growing trust.

Aiming to understand the interpretations and perspectives of another and then using that understanding to guide our actions is how we practice empathy in action, which is defined as "understanding, being aware of, being sensitive to, and vicariously experiencing the feelings, thoughts... of another... without having the feelings, thoughts, and experience fully communicated in an objectively explicit manner." Understanding someone's perspective, feeling what they're feeling, and then sensing what the other person might need from you are all component parts of effectively practicing empathy. This is the Observe-Experience-Amplify cycle I introduced in chapter 1.

As we've seen in previous chapters, intentional listening, carefully designing and making agreements, and active commitment management are all part of a stronger management approach. In order to sustain the power-with structure we're hoping to implement, we must learn to engage active empathy. Everyone involved benefits from you enriching your practice of empathy. Understanding our workplace as a network of systems, as a web of requests and commitments, means engaging with coworkers as if you could be in their shoes. If the structure is designed to be power-with, how the people around you feel becomes important and, to some extent, reflective of how you may come to feel.

Admittedly, engaging actively with empathy at work may feel daunting. There is enough to do in a day, and calling your emotions into the equation can seem like the last thing you need. However, good leaders engage their empathetic ability often; it is part of what makes them effective at elaborating on a task in such a way that highlights its meaning or importance. Remaining emotionally present at work offers a better way to engage.

Empathy Increases Our Innovation Capability

Jerry Hirshberg, the former president of Nissan Design, used to tell a story of the value of empathy in design and innovation. He was driving along a freeway one day when he saw something that made him stop. A competitor's minivan was pulled over to the side of the road, and a couple was wrestling out its back seat. Why? "We bought this so we would have room," they told him, "but we can't use it for what we want without taking out the seats." They needed to fit a new couch into it. They would never have thought of asking for any solution to their problem, but one immediately occurred to Hirshberg—six-foot runners that would enable van owners to fold up the back seats and slide them out of the way, thus easily creating cargo room.

This kind of empathy, which guides us towards innovation that has a widespread impact, has been called "empathic design" by Dorothy Leonard and Jeffrey Rayport in the *Harvard Business Review*: "The techniques of empathic design—gathering, analyzing, and applying information gleaned from observation in the field—are familiar to top engineering/design companies and to a few forward-thinking manufacturers, but they are not common practice." Additionally, a focus on Human Innovation calls for us to build shared values. Developing mutually important values is like a collective declaration that allows us to assess the effectiveness of our actions, or our level of satisfaction. Empathic design demands this. The higher level of empathy necessitated by Human Innovation not only observes but seeks areas where empathy can clue us into how to push the envelope. A higher level of empathy can allow for a higher level of innovation.

Toyota Research Institute has been developing a sensitive domestic robot. A future in which a robot opens your pickle jar is nearer than you might expect. The company reports, "As part of its work to create a domestic robot, TRI is focusing on innovating the machine's 'helping hands.' A domestic robot's hands (also known as manipulators or grippers) must handle a wide variety of household objects to be useful. These manipulators must be capable of stable grasps, precise placement, and safe interactions during inadvertent contact. To be affordable as part of a household robot, the gripper must also be low cost. TRI researchers have designed a manipulator with all these capabilities called the Soft Bubble Gripper." Key to further developing this machine's "helping hands" was a high degree of sensitivity in its gripping abilities. Toyota Research Institute made an effort to consider more sensitive populations while developing its domestic robot technology.

This kind of innovation demands a refined ability to practice empathy. And on a fundamental level, innovation is a powerful offer.

Empathy builds on the practice of developing conditions of satisfaction. It brings that listening to an even higher level and provides an even more powerful approach for designing offers and powerful innovations.

I have already outlined the ways a project allows us to practice developing networked commitments. Conditions of satisfaction with a customer, whatever kind of customer, allow for a higher level of agility than procedures in which we are not trying to reimagine the potential outcome or redesign a whole area of practice. But beyond conditions of satisfaction lies the deeper listening of empathy. Practiced empathy gives us the opportunity to innovate in a way that mutually conceived conditions cannot. To quote that much-referenced (though possibly apocryphal) Henry Ford quote, "If I asked my customers what they wanted, they would say a faster horse." Co-invention of conditions of satisfaction can certainly lay the foundation for deeper listening and for building trust, but empathy—having a sense of what the customer truly needs—is the foundation for great design.

My team and I were working with a division of a major global computer software and hardware manufacturing and development company committed to becoming a more services-oriented company. Our job was to help them move from order takers of hardware to consultative sellers of services—a significant change in mindset. We were prototyping with a pilot team.

I was coaching one of the senior executives, and he confided in me that his wife and daughters liked him more now that he knew how to listen. He was almost in tears; the emotional relief of being recognized for being empathetic with people he loved was so overwhelming. I was not coaching him on his personal life, but he had taken this new practice of becoming empathy-led home. With that level of embodiment and commitment, I knew that we had substantially increased the chances of success and sustainability for our work. This pilot team went from last on the list in sales to being number one in the region.

Language Is the Key to Empathy

Empathy is a hugely powerful (and often overlooked) tool for eliciting change within an organization. The core of empathy is how you use language. Through empathy, we can develop deeper understanding, unlock a deeper level of communication, and have greater impact.

Remember in chapter 3 when I was talking about overwhelm, I gave the example of a bank where the commercial bankers and the document processors couldn't communicate with each other? This was at one of America's largest banks, and it was losing deals and customers at an alarming rate. One of the biggest issues facing this division was a lack of empathy. The two groups on either side of the commercial lending division—the white, middle-class, college-educated men, and the women of color with high-school diplomas who had learned English as a second language—were clashing culturally at their cores.

If we had taken a problem-based approach to this issue, we might have hired an expert on team culture and empathy. But it would have taken us decades to help them empathize with each other if we had started by teaching them about empathy and then asked them to practice that at work. They might have thought that it was fascinating and relevant and inspiring, but they would have promptly forgotten it as soon as the next fire drill happened, and someone started yelling at someone else.

Instead, we introduced them to a pragmatic branch of design thinking called the Language/Action Perspective (LAP), which effectively shows people how to enact and practice agency: action by a human being to produce their desired outcome. The LAP leverages language to help people become designers of their own lives.

As Terry Winograd wrote, "Language is action. Through their linguistic acts people effect change in the world." Without language, we might be able to develop empathy, but it would take a very long time, we would not be able to do much else at the same time, and we would certainly not be able to find design solutions to complex problems. We couldn't create opportunities, negotiate outcomes, or collaborate on innovative solutions. By using the LAP, the commercial bankers and document processors were able to develop a new shared framework for coordination. They had a shared understanding of the problems in the process. They were able to negotiate and together design shared standards for satisfaction for each other and for their customers. They were ultimately able to develop empathy by listening well enough to each other to collaborate and build trust.

The document processors developed a sufficient level of agency that they gained the respect of the commercial bankers. As a result, the combined group's customer satisfaction ratings, as measured by an outside body, jumped 11 percent, unheard of in the history of the department's measurements.

But best of all, at least for me: one of the document processors confided in me that she no longer cried on the way to work. That's empathy in the trenches. All good design begins with empathy.

In a sense, they were able to speak the same language, which allowed them to gain a deep and empathetic understanding of the problems they were facing for the first time.

Empathy is essential, but it's not enough by itself, and that wasn't the full solution for the problem at the bank. Although empathy is an important starting point for innovation—giving us the inspiration we need to understand the nature of problems deeply—inspiration itself doesn't innovate. When we are firmly rooted in our understanding of the customer, their agency, and their position in the hierarchy of processes, we can speculate about how to serve the customer better. At the same time, we must remember that the network of conversations happens both inside and outside the company. We must also not forget that conversations between humans do not always acknowledge the boundaries constructed to define individual companies, customers, or employees.

With this foundation, we begin to recognize, design, and model conversations to produce customer satisfaction in every conversation that we have both inside and outside the company. People transform from "inbox processors" with mind-numbing tasks for disembodied managers and departments to human designers and performers of requests, offers, and mutual promises to other human beings. The human, or social, work gains meaning as goals, visions, and a desire to satisfy customers come to life.

Once we have this solidly in place, we enter the magical realm of co-invention. The design thinking model refers to this as *ideation*. But as anyone who has done ideation knows, the result is only as good as the participants' level of mutual trust and willingness to play and learn together. I call this the magical realm because it's really where the magic happens, again and again. This realm is where human beings get to invent something better together, where we have fun and really get to know each other. By that, I don't mean knowing what someone's dog ate for breakfast or the names and ages of their kids. I'm talking about knowing how another person thinks, what they value, how they see the world, what matters to them, and how we can engage in delivering value for each other.

A Commitment to Mastery

I have introduced you to trust and empathy as cornerstone practices that support your six steps to building your own and others' innovation capacity. Mastery is the third very powerful pillar to support you.

To many people, *mastery* is a daunting prospect. However, a commitment to research and innovation already places you on the path to mastery. The kind of research and personal development that comes from reading and thinking about your field can help guide you towards mastery.

When I talk about mastery, I mean it in the sense Hubert Dreyfus defined in his levels of learning. What I love about Dreyfus's model is that he offers us a path to mastery through practice from beginner at the bottom of the ladder to master at the top—not so we become experts but so we remain humble practitioners on a lifelong path to mastery.

Dreyfus taught philosophy at MIT and UC Berkeley. He is well known for his decades-long critique of artificial intelligence that culminated in *What Computers Still Can't Do*. He developed what has since become the standard for understanding levels of learning, which gives us a powerful, actionable definition of master—a way to set a direction for ourselves.

We might wonder what this looks like, or how we could go about developing a practice of mastery to reinvent a discipline. Consider any physical practice—running, tennis, or yoga. Oftentimes we are content to remain a beginner or an advanced beginner in those areas. Maybe we want to become a yoga teacher, so we take a yoga teacher training course, which moves us to the competent level. This skill then becomes something we could monetize: we become a practitioner. Beyond this level, the margins shrink and the difference between a virtuoso and a master become both all the more minute and all the more evident.

Hubert Dreyfus's Levels of Learning

Master	Reinvents the discipline.
Virtuoso	Observes the direction of the discipline and can adapt new research to better satisfy customers.
Practitioner	Meets standards of excellence commonly shared by the community and recurrently produces customer satisfaction.
Competent	Can apply the distinctions and produce useful business results.
Advanced beginner	Can apply the basic principles to simple problems and understands what to study next.
Beginner	Has identified the basic definition of the field of practice.

Let's think for a moment of E.O. Wilson, who was one of the world's leading authorities on ant societies, evolution, and sociobiology. He asserted that *consilience*, a term of his own design, has occurred across a broad range of the natural sciences—from physics and chemistry to geology, molecular biology, and biochemistry. For Wilson, certainly a master in his domain, consilience meant massive cross-disciplinary knowledge leaps within the sciences. Few of us are in the arena of reinvention, as Wilson was. However, now we at least understand the path. The beginner who is determined and committed to becoming at least a practitioner builds a path for themselves to higher levels of learning, before ultimately committing themselves to contribute to the discipline. And as we become proficient in an area, we aspire to change the discipline, but we must humbly acknowledge that that may never happen.

Obviously, you can't be masterful at everything. It is hard to be masterful at many things. You can also deliberately choose *not* to be masterful in certain domains. You can instead choose to be a beginner, advanced beginner, or competent. As a wise friend of mine would often say, "Not my mountain to climb. Not my work to do." If you look at tools and practices as supporting your own mastery, you become a lot more selective, discriminating, and deliberate in your learning.

If you try to take on too many disciplines, you are likely to become jack of all trades but master of none—the Swiss Army knife of all work. Wouldn't you rather be operated on by a surgeon who uses an orthoscopic instrument rather than a Swiss Army knife?

Each Domain Can Contribute to the Others

Mastery is not hyperspecialization. Someone who is committed to hyperspecialization seeks to know everything there is to know (obviously impossible) about a certain topic, at the expense of knowledge in any other topic. Someone who commits to mastery in a certain domain commits to reinventing the discipline. This demands that you live in a constant state of inquiry, of humble beginner mind, of passionate learning, because you are constantly scanning the horizon—as far as you can see—for the next perturbation, which might lead to the next moonshot, to the next breakthrough innovation. And you are honest enough to accept that you don't know where it will come from. You may have a sense or a hunch— and you have the courage to follow it.

And choosing a domain to focus on and develop mastery in does not mean being unskilled in all other domains. Skills and practices are actually portable from one domain to another and can help another domain develop.

For example, if I get competent at cooking, one of the things that I will have learned to do is mise en place. This means "putting things in place" in French, and it is a very effective practice in cooking: laying out all your ingredients and equipment before you begin to cook. It's also an approach and mental skill that I use in many other domains from home repair to project management. After all, as Benjamin Franklin said, "Failing to prepare is preparing to fail."

Similarly, if you are a piano player, you may have a practice of sitting down and reading a piece of music from beginning to end before you ever touch the keys. This is a powerful practice for feeling your way into the music—and it's also very portable practice for listening to other people, reading papers, understanding projects before you dive into action, and many other domains of mastery.

In addition, practices that masters in other domains have developed can support your pursuit of mastery in your own domain. You don't have to become masterful in that other domain, but you can certainly use their tools and practices. For example, the practice of breathing and grounding your- self in yoga is very useful when you observe yourself getting triggered by someone who needs to be right. This breathing practice can be adapted to listening and co-inventing, and it often allows you to find a possibility for progress, instead of conflict. In chapter 1, I said that one of the responsibilities of a leader is to help others build more powerful interpretations; people's backgrounds and interpretations of the world allow them to take certain actions. When they can see a more powerful interpretation, they can embody new competence. We are now doing that for ourselves with practices by recognizing many different domains of human achievement and levels of learning.

Once you recognize levels of learning in your own and other domains, you get to decide what level you wish to accomplish.

Empathy, Mastery, and Interdisciplinary Innovation

E.O. Wilson argued that consilience—the "'jumping together' of knowledge" across disciplines "to create a common groundwork of explanation"—is the most promising path to scientific advancement, intellectual adventure, and human awareness. Wilson and other interdisciplinary advocates contend that the breaching of scientific boundaries will lead to breakthroughs as critical as the cracking of the DNA code. Wilson believed that an interdisciplinary approach to knowledge development is essential for advancing our thinking. This idea gets to the core of something equally relevant inside work and our own development: if we want to make great strides, advance in leaps and bounds, an interdisciplinary practice is critical.

Mastery, although at first glance a process of specialization, can actually allow for a higher level of interdisciplinary involvement. When we are particularly clear about what we offer to ourselves, our workplace, or the world writ large, we are all the better equipped to collaborate and co-invent. As we discussed earlier, innovation is always a deeply powerful offer. Committing to engage in mastery as a practice, and consequently minimizing the scope of your commitments, allows you to search out expertise and ask questions. This encourages you to engage differently. Suddenly, everyone involved in a different field or with a different avenue of mastery is an adjacent practitioner, not a competitor. When we practice mastery humbly and mindfully, we are competing not against another person but against a *standard* of mastery. Someone who is masterful in a different arena can become infinitely more valuable to us, and a much better teacher, when we can justly regard them as a coconspirator on our path to enhancing our own practice. This mental orientation will inevitably foster collaboration. We become all the more aware of what we can learn from others around us.

Additionally, the necessary acknowledgment that we may never arrive at a complete level of mastery can be somewhat softened by interdisciplinary collaboration. Like E.O. Wilson suggested, that is where a breakthrough is more likely to happen. And if anything, this is a deeply human tendency, which the arsenal of tools we have developed throughout the course of this book help to make interdisciplinary collaboration easier.

Empathy and mastery both engage our highest levels of listening and practice. We are all the more likely to arrive at something like a moonshot, some kind of discontinuous innovation, when we engage actively and consciously with other committed practitioners. How many of us can think of an instance when something someone has said, totally unrelated to your own area of work, has sparked a new and creative idea for you? Isn't it always the case that you're doing something like listening to a podcast about the world's best mountain biking when an idea related to your latest work challenge seems to just click into place?

Deep recognition and development of your own mastery establishes you as a more astute observer of the mastery of others. It also helps you to be more appreciative and respectful of the effort required. You will find that that these qualities invite others in pursuit of mastery to engage more openly with you.

Over time, as we use our capacity of listening, making offers, negotiating, and managing commitments to deliberately build trust with others, we also position ourselves to be more empathetic. From this powerful point of empathy, we also create space for our own mastery to grow, and we increase our ability to observe and appreciate the mastery of others. And we become more attuned to our ability to adopt practices from other domains, so we continue to grow our own mastery. This puts us in the sweet spot of deeply respecting mastery outside our own discipline and sets us up for interdisciplinary innovation.

Key Practice: Declare Your Domain

Write down answers for these three questions:

1 What is the domain in which you commit to developing mastery for yourself? (Declare it! You can always change your mind later.)

2 What are the tools and practices from other domains that will serve you in pursuit of your mastery?

3 What level of learning do you wish to attain in the tools and practices that support your own mastery?

Identify your current supporting practices and look at other practices that you have in other domains of your life or that you have seen others use. See how over time you can build out a portfolio of powerful practices to support your pursuit of mastery. For example, if your area of mastery is autonomous driving perception, you might have the following practices to support your mastery: design thinking, agile project management, and human innovation. You might also have the following tools: coding platforms, research databases, literature search tools, and others that come from other domains of mastery. And if you become an astute observer of mastery, you may also have advisors, friends, or allies who are masterful in these domains and can support you in your primary domain.

Life is easier and a lot more enjoyable when you are surrounded by others committed to mastery in your own and other domains. It gives you a newfound respect for others' commitments as you realize how big a lift it is for you.

6

Creating Knowledge

or, When the Whole Is Greater Than the Sum of the Parts

"The hardest thing I have had to learn as a CEO is the ability to manage my own psychology."
BEN HOROWITZ

YOU KNOW more than you know you know—and that fact is essential to helping you create even more knowledge.

I'll explain. Knowledge can be divided into two types. Tacit knowledge is knowledge that that you're not always aware of having. It's the valuable and highly subjective insight and intuition that is difficult to capture and share. If you play a musical instrument, play a sport, practice yoga or a martial art, you already know that tacit knowledge exists in our bodies—in our reflexes, nervous systems, and trained responses. Explicit knowledge, on the other hand, is formal and systematic. It can be easily communicated and distributed through product specifications, scientific formulas, blueprints and technical specifications, or computer programs. Professors Nonaka and Takeuchi defined and popularized the distinction in their work and book, *The Knowledge-Creating Company*.

We think of explicit knowledge as being the fuel of our cognition, but Nonaka and Takeuchi recognize that tacit knowledge has a significant cognitive dimension. It consists of mental models, beliefs, and perspectives ingrained in our common sense. It is the things we often take for granted, so it's harder to articulate. But it's real, and we rely on it. Someone practicing something specific, related to their domain, has a level of knowledge beyond information—a level of knowledge that is deeply embodied and much more nuanced.

Although we might think of ourselves as logical beings, embodied knowledge is different, more organic. A surgeon, in the middle of an incredibly delicate operation, might request a scalpel, and the attending nurse will know exactly what to look for and when to give it to her. It's these moments that become embodied as practices. This is a shared understanding and shared knowledge. These coworkers have created knowledge between the two of them over hundreds of surgeries.

Anyone who has worked in innovation or aspires to be an innovator knows that the process of research, investigation, and ideation is part science and part art. By being aware of this, we can exercise our practices to work with both the science and the art to create higher levels and higher value knowledge. If our work is designed in a state of power-with, how we feel about the people around us becomes important, and to some extent, reflective. Mutual respect, empathy, and commitment-based engagement and management practices cultivate trust. We are laying the foundation that allows us to fine-tune our own areas of mastery. As we develop our abilities to empathize and to rely consistently on our network of commitments, we develop room for growth in our own mastery. Taking this human innovation approach frees up space.

In this chapter, we will explore the knowledge creation process to enable the artist and the innovator within each of us to create knowledge together. We will also explore how to understand and intentionally and systematically cultivate our capacity to make knowledge explicit. By learning to do this, we can engage more effectively with others while recognizing when our often highly intuitive tacit knowledge can be brought to the forefront and honored, appreciated, and valued. This process is the fifth step—create knowledge—in growing our innovation capacity.

The Six Step Practice Model

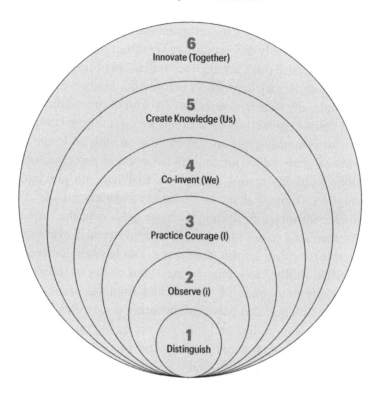

Information Is Not Knowledge

Our education system relies heavily on the digestion and regurgitation of information. Memorization and the ability to recite information are often the determining factors in getting good grades, which we treat as synonymous with intelligence. Culturally, there is a dominant image of the human mind as a computer that takes in and puts out facts. There used to be entire categories of jobs in data entry, where the human was in service to a machine. Data meant the machine could function, generate reports, do calculations, and facilitate searches. Though we have imagined our brains as computers, they are obviously different: there are things humans do that computers still can't simulate accurately, and things that we use computers to do precisely because our brains won't. For example, although computers save us a lot of time in drafting and doing engineering calculations, we can't rely on computers for something like artistic expression with an irregular physical material, or for conceptualization of potential solutions to highly complex problems that have no previous solution. Thinking about our brains as computers ignores our innate advantage in dealing with the unknown, the unpredictable. And so does thinking that computers will ever fully be able to replace human intelligence. Our biological, diverse, creative abilities as human beings—our ability to translate creativity into material, visual, and linguistic artifacts— make us unique and powerful inventors of our own future.

When you understand this, you recognize that creating knowledge is an organic process. And you know that information is not knowledge—but it is very useful in the creation of knowledge.

If you are committed to understanding how to create knowledge to better innovate, how do you identify, understand, value, and leverage different kinds of knowledge? How do you discern which type of knowledge might lead to a breakthrough in your thinking? How do you know what sort of knowledge is needed in a stalled conversation? How do you know who to bring into the conversation or how to set up the type of conversation that will be most useful? How do you open yourself up to a richer understanding of how to engage with the knowledge around you? Can you include knowledge your most unlikely colleague might potentially contribute?

The Knowledge/Intention Matrix is a useful guide to engaging in intentional conversations for knowledge creation. It identifies four modes, which I have named apprentice, technician, artist, and innovator.

The Knowledge/Intention Matrix

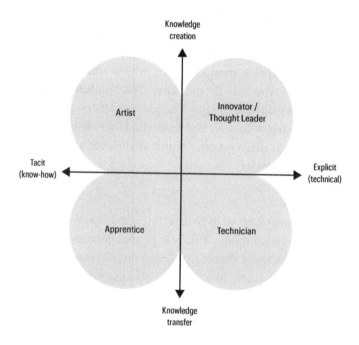

The horizontal axis measures whether the knowledge is tacit or explicit. The vertical axis measures the use, intent, or purpose in engaging with knowledge. At one end is knowledge transfer. Are you looking to transfer the knowledge to another group, department, OEM? Is it one-to-one or on a bigger scale? Do you need to apply knowledge to solve a particular problem?

At the other end is knowledge creation. Are you seeking to create new knowledge? Are you pursuing a breakthrough in your understanding or that of your team? Or are you chasing a moonshot to change people's lives for the better?

Apprentice

When you are involved in transferring tacit knowledge, you are in apprentice mode. Apprenticeship requires time with the master to observe, practice, inquire, and note patterns and anomalies. Those who are best at apprentice mode know how to apprentice themselves to others and to serve and grow others who may do the same. They understand knowledge is not information and that great teachers and trainers share their passion, love, and embodied knowledge with others. You need them on your team, as they are the nodes for knowledge transfer.

Technician

When you are involved in transferring explicit knowledge, you are in technician mode. The best people here leverage information to increase their knowledge but are less concerned with teaching others than applying information systematically and rigorously. With their focused technical expertise, these people are often lab managers and machine repair experts who can fix, repair, and calibrate quickly and efficiently. They are technical writers and blueprint developers. The brilliant bike repair guy who diagnosed and fixed a strange little problem with my bike in five minutes is a master technician.

Artist

In the realm of the artist and the innovator, you're working with tacit and explicit knowledge while creating new knowledge. Creating knowledge is both organic and emergent. The artist works more with tacit knowledge. They can do amazing things and produce great results, but because they work in the realm of tacit knowledge, in order to transfer or create knowledge, they need to work either with an apprentice or with another artist at their level of complexity and maturity of expression.

Innovator or Thought Leader

An innovator (as a person or team of people) brings forth their knowledge as products, services, or experiences, which result in the adoption of new practices in a community. To do that, they must first make their knowledge explicit, available, and usable by a larger number of people. Think of the entire Apple ecosystem: coders, developers, designers, product designers, engineers, sales and marketing people. Knowledge is made explicit across the network of commitments, all across the ecosystem through innovation and thought leadership.

In reality, these axes are a spectrum. As always in life, humans encompass a range, even though we distinguish conceptually between modes. If you truly commit yourself to mastery in knowledge creation and innovation or thought leadership, you will ideally flex across the modes to engage effectively with whomever you are working.

These highly complex, ingrained models profoundly shape how we perceive, interpret, and innovate in the world. That means the most effective thing you can do when innovating with another human being is to listen.

Listening for Creating Knowledge

When listening to create knowledge, you are not just listening to what is being said. You are more than two eardrums

Depths of Listening

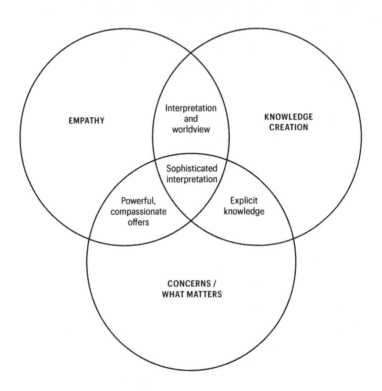

receiving and processing moving air molecules. You are a highly complex, emergent, adaptive human being listening for the mental models, beliefs, perspectives, and interpretations of another human being. And this happens while you are observing and reflecting on your own mental models, beliefs, perspectives, and interpretations and how they are interacting positively or negatively with your knowledge creation partner. You are working in highly dense, complex feedback loops. The more you can distinguish them, the better you can observe them, and the better you can listen.

As I stated earlier, anyone who has been focused on innovation for a long time appreciates that it is part science and a whole lot of art. One of the most powerful levers for the art is listening. There are three depths of listening that can drive innovation:

1 Listening for concerns
2 Empathetic listening
3 Listening for knowledge creation

If you're serious about innovating with another human, and you want to become a sincere practitioner, listening is essential. Listening is remarkably like love. To love others or be loved by them, we have to start with ourselves—and that is always easier said than done. It's pretty much the same with listening. When committing to being a good listener, the best place to start is by listening to yourself.

Listening for Concerns

The first type of listening is listening for concerns and what matters. We have already seen the levels of concern we need to listen for in chapter 3 with the Listening for Concerns matrix.

This is important, and you will need to return to it again and again. It is the essence of knowing what matters to you. It allows you to listen deeply to what matters to others with appreciation and respect. I always ask people I work with to take notes using the Listening for Concerns matrix. It can be a daunting task and take months of practice to do effectively, but it is the most powerful starting point. You will build many such matrices depending on the circumstances. The more proficient you are at listening to your own and others' concerns, the more agile you will be at making offers and requests to take care of these concerns.

Listening for Concerns

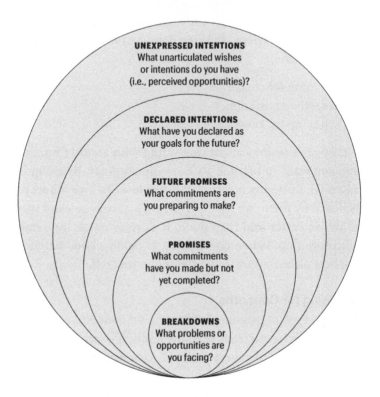

When you have a powerful handle on what matters to you, the next step is to engage in networks and commitments to take care of what matters to others. It's reciprocal: what matters to you matters to others, and what matters to others matters to you. Take care of those concerns at all different levels. That doesn't mean you go into every interaction with an agenda. It means you pay attention to everyone's concerns as you make offers and mutual promises to deliver on those commitments. A mutual exchange of listening, caring, and commitment leads to opportunities to innovate successfully together and accomplish something more than anyone could do individually. The sum of the whole truly becomes greater than the parts.

Empathetic Listening

The next level of listening is empathy. In chapter 5, I talked about empathy and how it can amplify our co-invention capacity. Combined, empathy and listening for concerns allow us to make powerful, compassionate offers. And we have discussed how these offers can be a generative engine of innovation within your team and your company. When we actively practice listening and engage and develop these capabilities, over time we develop deeper listening capabilities and become more aware and practiced at the art and science of knowledge creation.

Listening for Knowledge Creation

If I'm listening for the purposes of creating knowledge, I've already done the listening to understand the person's concerns, I've done some work to understand their perspective and worldview, and I'm interested in building empathy for them and with them in order to actively create knowledge with them. I need to understand how they see the world: What are their interpretations? What are the lenses they use to make sense of their work, their situation, their desires and ambitions? What distinctions between words or between ideas matter to them, and why do they consider these distinctions to be important? The more I can understand this about them and about myself, the easier it is for me to identify our points of shared passion. I'm doing that level of listening all of the time, but I'm doing it not for the purpose of making offers—I'm doing it to understand how this person sees the world and how that influences how they act and make decisions. In this way, I'm creating knowledge about them with their help. It's a tremendous honor.

Consciously building more sophisticated interpretations is at the intersection of listening for what matters, empathy, and knowledge creation. As one of my brilliantly insightful clients said, "90 percent of innovation is finding the right question." The more sophisticated your interpretations, in your selected domain of mastery, the better the questions you can ask. I urge you to start observing this for yourself. When you hear someone saying something that you find truly insightful, ask yourself, Is it because they know more or because they know enough to ask better questions? Do they curate, cultivate, and husband their interpretations more effectively than I do? Do they courageously and intentionally make powerful, compassionate offers to further their inquiry and to increase the sophistication of their interpretations?

Once you acknowledge that increasing the sophistication of your interpretations supports you in listening and creating knowledge more powerfully, you can see how to increase your innovation capacity.

Amplifying Others

To lead innovation effectively, we need to learn how to amplify others. You're listening, engaging, making offers, and co-inventing. You have created networks of commitments and relationships and are managing them. But as a leader, you are responsible for bringing the most out of your team and your customers, to step up their capacity as well as yours. You need to amplify them.

I introduced the concept of amplifying others and the Three Engines of Capacity Development (or the Observe-Experience-Amplify model) in chapter 1. Through exploring this and unpacking the Six Step Practice Model, you are set to create the innovation mindset for yourself, your team, and the ecosystem in which you work.

The old view is that a worker has been brought in to do work, which they assume means input-process-output: they take requests and give results. It may be that nobody has ever said to them, "You are here because you are intelligent. You are here because you are capable. You are here because I want you to engage. You are here because I want you to bring your innovative and co-inventive capacity to our company. That is where you are most valuable."

The Three Engines of Capacity Development

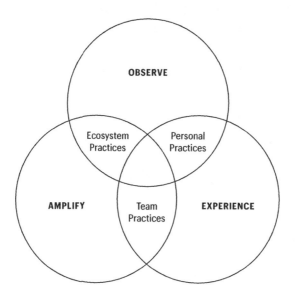

When you enable people to see a more powerful interpretation of work, they can embody a new competence. Our job as leaders, particularly as leaders of human innovation, is how we help people build more powerful interpretations, ones that we can lend to them, ones that they can embody and build on themselves. From there, we help them embody new competence, relying on the fact that people are good at learning and derive enormous satisfaction in taking care of each other. We've set up a world of work in which we believe without question that we can't do that, so one of the most important and simplest levers for starting this transformation is to help people understand that they need to be asking, "Why am I doing this?"

We've been brought up to do what we're told. We tend to follow procedures, produce deliverables, follow the company line, march to the core for the results of expectations. We work between nine and five and follow those boundaries as much as we possibly can, and we live for the weekend. We've never been given permission to or trained to ask ourselves, "What is this person asking me to do? How is it valuable for them? What do they care about?" If I listen to others to understand what matters to them and what their concerns are, and I focus on developing an understanding of what matters to me, I can develop a deeper understanding of how to engage in co-invention with my customer.

Our ability to take care of our own concerns in the world as well as our ability to take care of the concerns of the people we work for is part of what builds our competence. I've witnessed many senior executive teams struggle under the weight of their work. They've never learned to amplify other human beings. They tend to look for more and more and more resources. If you amplify and elevate and leverage the talent you already have, you might find that you are more efficient and have more space and more room and more time in your day.

Part of this process is moving yourself out of coping. Many of us spend a huge percentage of our time in a state of coping, and we don't train our team to take stuff off our plate. By listening to us and co-inventing our own futures as well as theirs, our team can better help us. You can engage with other people to create something that's bigger than both of you.

The way to do that is to start engaging your team in the process of co-invention. And it means engaging your whole team and ensuring that team has as many different perspectives as possible.

The Maker-Creator Spectrum

One important difference in perspective is found in the kinds of innovators, a spectrum that I suggest spans the maker at one end and the creator at the other. Most of us likely sit somewhere between the two, vacillating between one role and the other depending on the context. Some of us more obviously sit on one side of the spectrum or the other; we are more clear-cut makers or creators. If we think about the list of qualities in the Maker-Creator Spectrum diagram and self-assess, it may become apparent to us what kind of innovation diversity we bring to our teams, our firms, and our specific roles.

The Maker-Creator Spectrum

Maker	Creator
Building	Listening
Engineering	Designing
Analyzing	Contextualizing
Problem-solving	Understanding
Investigating	Inspiring
Isolating	Connecting
Narrowing focus	Framing

Makers and creators focus on different things and find themselves more immediately curious about different problems and opportunities. If we are attuned to our own avenues of mastery, we can better attend to the kind of innovation we bring to our workplace and teams. We can ask ourselves, What kind of innovator am I? After placing ourselves on this spectrum, we are more likely to understand our own areas of focus.

To better flesh out the distinction between maker and creator, we can think about products and systems, both discussed earlier. Business often has a product-driven focus: we look for output as a marker of success. Although this is a more traditional model, it still has its place. In a moment of innovation, the more product-driven maker plays an important role in the process. We come to recognize this kind of innovation drive when we look for the individuals focused on the specifics. These are the meticulous people we rely on when a specific functional problem needs a discrete resolution. Leadership from this place on the spectrum might look more like the now notorious idea to plop "shade balls" into the Los Angeles reservoir, which are designed to slow decreasing water levels and stall the aggressive drought facing California. It's a highly specific problem with a gadget-driven solution—one that doesn't necessarily look beyond its scope (for example, at the amount of water used in producing the balls, or other effects the balls might have on bacterial growth and aquatic life).

In some respects, the creators on our teams are more difficult to spot, and our traditional business structures are less capable of recognizing the benefit of these people. Although their work is perhaps less immediately obvious, creators are no less critically important. Skills like listening, designing, and contextualizing are generally underrated outside work, and they are both underrated and particularly underleveraged inside a workplace. I have written at length about the benefit of designing our own work, listening to the concerns of others, and trying to understand the network of requests. This kind of focus sheds light for us on the benefit of the role of creator. As we look at the benefits of using our own sense of designing and listening, we can better identify how the creator can lead us towards innovation.

The difference between these types of innovators can lead us to the kind of co-invention that sparks innovation. If we are driven to innovate, we need the whole spectrum between these two poles. We need the creative tension it creates as a driver of innovation. Different kinds of diversity allow for this kind of creative tension. We can intentionally pursue that diversity and develop that creative tension within our teams.

Leveraging the Genius of Gender Balance

As we take the final step to innovating together, I want to look for a moment at one particularly powerful way of amplifying others and pursuing diversity for cocreation. The more perspectives we have, the more we can cocreate and innovate. Yet the dominant voices in work have for a long time been more similar to one another than they need to be. Gender balance is a key example of this. Evidence suggests that a diversity of gender drives innovation and has financial incentives. To quote an article from EY Americas, "Boards with at least 30 percent women have higher profit margins than those who don't—we now see increasing evidence linking diversity to innovation, which is critical to successfully navigating disruption in this transformation age." There is also a less visible component: this kind of diversity can lead to innovation through unexpected avenues.

What is it about gender diversity that facilitates innovation? Research done by EY Americas, a global management consulting firm, confirms that it's the plurality of views:

"Innovation that uncovers new paths to growth will only spring from high-performing, gender-diverse teams that maximize the power of different opinions, perspectives, and cultural references." This research reminds us that a difference of perspectives is part of what drives creativity. Different opinions and perspectives push us in new directions. Diversity can spark innovation. If we are seeking newness that comes from delivering innovation, gender diversity is one ingredient that can help us get there. The Center for Talent Innovation "found that companies with gender balanced teams are 70 percent more likely to capture new markets and 75 percent more likely to get innovative ideas to market. Evidence also suggests diversity leads to improved outcomes."

Gender Diversity Is a Powerful Corporate Performance Lever

Firms that lead on gender balance enjoy measurably superior performance across seven business imperatives.

1. Innovation	76% more likely to get innovative ideas to market
2. Decision-making	Better decisions 78% of the time, and twice as quickly
3. Risk reduction	24% fewer governance controversies per US$B in market cap
4. Customer experience	27% more likely to create longer term customer value
5. Employee engagement	18% higher levels of team commitment
6. Operational excellence	Two additional percentage points of EBITDA
7. Strategy	70% more likely to successfully identify and capture new markets

Key Practice: Helping People Move from Coping to Creating

This key practice is a set of group activities taken from my Next Level Innovations Leaders program, in which we focus on helping leaders build their capacity to amplify others and reduce the risk of burnout.

Conversation Timeline
- Activity 1: Declaring Standards: 10 minutes
- Activity 2: Current Realities: 20 minutes
- Activity 3: Setting New Standards: 20 minutes
- Activity 4: Wrap Up and Action Steps: 10 minutes

Activity 1: Declaring Standards
Required time: 10 minutes
Note to Conversation Leaders: While the group may strongly agree that high standards are important, they may struggle with understanding their role in setting standards when they are the performer, particularly if they have been given standards to meet previously (and don't have an issue with it). Help shift their thinking by emphasizing how the pace of change means taking ownership for establishing standards and being able to reconnect through the work effort if elements change.

Prep Work
Each person should come to the conversation having read chapter 4.

Introduction for the Group
Put the following in your own words:

- The pace of change today means static standards of work aren't effective; both parties need to take an active role early in the conversation to ensure that work standards are discussed and are clear and feasible.

- Without clear standards, there's a risk of overwork or rework; minimizing this risk is critical, given the pace and volume of work we continue to manage.

- These standards must be clear. (There are examples in chapter 4.)

- It is no longer sufficient for standards to be communicated by the customer; co-inventing the conditions of satisfaction means performers need to be involved in declaring standards early, and not wait for them to be defined.

Questions for the Group (3–5 minutes)
- What resonated most for you in chapter 4?

- Where are clear standards for working together needed? Do you see the connection to increased pace of work, and why this is important?

- How does our new language for managing shared commitments impact setting standards for our work? Do you agree that the urgency for creating standards up front as we make commitments has changed? Why or why not?

Activity 2: Current Realities

Required time: 20 minutes

Introduction for the Group

Put the following in your own words:

- We're going to start by talking about where differences in work standards between the customer (the person requesting the work) and the performer are an issue.

- Identifying the situations where new language and ownership for co-inventing standards is most critical is our first step.

Questions to Discuss as a Full Group (10–15 minutes)

Let's talk about situations where there are unclear or differing standards—whether we're the customer or performer. Examples are customer satisfaction, making offers, project quality, managing commitments, etc.

- Are there existing standards we're using today? Are there gaps or inconsistencies in how we define our work standards for ourselves and our work? Where do you see this happening? *(Write these on the whiteboard.)*

- Why is this an issue? Who is impacted? What happens (or doesn't happen) when different standards exist?

- Are there new standards of work we've defined or created since our initial workshop? What progress have we made so far? Is everyone on the same page, or are some moving at a different pace, which is creating different standards or expectations?

Activity 3: Setting New Standards
Required time: 20 minutes
Required supplies: Pen, paper, whiteboard, and markers

Introduction for the Group
Put the following in your own words:

- One of the challenges for teams can be adopting shared language and processes in step with each other.

- When change is about aligned standards for outcomes, open conversations about what this means and how the work will evolve are even more critical.

Questions to Discuss as a Full Group (10–15 minutes)

- Are there common standards for certain situations that we can agree to as a group?

- How does establishing shared standards work in a network of commitments, as we discussed previously? *(Give some space for this part of the discussion before moving on.)*

- Where will your own work benefit from an opportunity to declare standards? Is there more ease of usage that you see as a customer versus as a performer?

- What language do we need to introduce to support early declaration of standards between individuals? Will this be difficult to do?

- What's going to get in our way? What happens if things don't change? How can we best support each other in making this happen?

Activity 4: Wrap Up and Action Steps

Required time: 10 minutes

Note to Conversation Leaders: This is where you bring it all together for the group and talk about how each person will choose something to work on over the next thirty days, as a first step towards improving how work is managed within the group.

Introduction for the Group

Put the following in your own words:

- The final piece in our conversation is to think about what we intend to do differently based on what we've learned and to commit to one practice over the next thirty days.

- As with the previous conversation, we'll support each other in making regular check-ins to meet our commitment goals.

Questions for the Group (5–10 minutes)

- What's one thing you plan to implement or do differently over the next thirty days as a result of our conversation today?

- What does success look like to you? How would your organization or industry benefit from this change?

- How can we support each other in achieving our commitments?

Commitments

They can choose one of the following commitments, or create their own:

- When I see repeated breakdowns occur with another team member, I will meet with them to understand if we have different standards for how the work should be done.

- If I see people who report to me struggling to coordinate and collaborate with each other, I will meet with them to see if they have articulated shared standards for working effectively together.

- When I see that we are wasting time, creating recurrent breakdowns, or frustrating each other, I will look at the process (the network of commitments) that we are working in and see if we need to redesign it with new standards.

Conclusion:
Three Levels of Innovation Capacity

NOW WE find ourselves at the top of the ladder, ready to innovate. It's time to come back to the three levels of innovation capacity that we saw at the beginning of the book. They show you how, as you practice the innovation mindset, you can map your progress from a motley crew of smart individuals to hopefully game-changing innovation superstars.

Level One: Commodity

Level One is the commodity level. This is for the uninformed, those with great hubris who believe that innovation is a commodity that can be bought by bringing together a bunch of smart people.

Startup culture in Silicon Valley creates the illusion that it is possible to take a bunch of smart people, a good idea, and some funding and create a unicorn company. Nothing could be further from the truth. About three-quarters of venture-capital-backed firms in the US don't return investors' capital, according to research by Shikhar Ghosh, a senior lecturer at Harvard Business School. Yes, that is a whopping 75 percent of VC-backed companies fail! What percentage of corporate-funded innovation projects fail? And how much money is invested by corporations in failed innovation efforts?

Ask any VC with a half-decent track record and they will tell you that they don't invest in the idea, they invest in the team. They are not investing in smart people with untested ideas who are burned out and don't have a clear critical path to revenue and scaling. As you can hopefully see for yourself, these problems are symptomatic of a lack of innovation mindset and its associated practices and accumulated skills.

Level Two: People

The name of this level cuts to the point of the issue: functional and robust innovation processes come from people. Investors, whether companies or venture firms, invest in people. They invest in people who know how to coordinate, co-invent, make offers, listen, create knowledge, distinguish and fine-tune practices, build common language and standards for knowledge creation, and establish partnerships across ecosystems for scaling and growth. You can have the best ideas and the best technologists in the business but if they don't know how to practice innovation, you lack a generative engine to drive your innovation capability.

Level Three: Ecosystem

With the capacity to engage and innovate through listening, partnerships, and the innovation mindset, you and your practices become amplifiers of the ecosystem. You begin to establish yourself as a leader with a shot at a moonshot. You attract top talent, the kind that money can't buy, people who want to know what you are up to, who want to apprentice to the masters—masters of the innovation mindset. From there, the moonshot is yours to attain.

A Final Pitch for Practices

The engine behind all of this is our ability to understand the power and value of practices, which I introduced in the beginning of the book as the Practice/Impact Model.

The Practice/Impact Model gives us a way to understand how the power of practices can support the development of our innovation capacity. It shows the increases in sophistication and impact as we move up the ladder from basic individual abilities to innovating with cross-functional and cross-disciplinary teams.

On the operational level, we begin with organic talents (x) and increase in sophistication to skills (2x) and competencies (4x). From there, we level up into the generative, starting with individual deliberate practices (20x). At that point, the increase in sophistication becomes collective, and we see richer conversations (60x), better design (70x), and ultimately agile co-inventive processes (100x).

As you cultivate your ability to observe powerful practices all around you, and you slowly and carefully build out your portfolio of practices on your way to mastery, you invariably share them and help others with theirs. It takes about six months to effectively embody a new practice. Over time, you become an engine of capacity development and move yourself and your team up the innovation capacity ladder distinguishing, observing, making courageous offers, co-inventing, creating knowledge, and innovating together, as you go. You become more sophisticated in your individual and collective interpretations and increase your chances of groundbreaking innovation! I very much look forward to being the beneficiary of some of your moonshots.

In celebration of how innovation and innovators enhance our lives,
Jennifer Kenny

Acknowledgments

BEGAN THIS book as a way to answer a question for myself, one that I have been asking for years. The people around me know firsthand that I live in the inquiry—how do we innovate better together? I am convinced that the future of innovation is interdisciplinary, gender balanced, and based on practices that allow us to move with agility and generativity in organizations that, in the future, will be managed as complex, adaptive systems. I am grateful for their shared curiosity and their generosity in assisting me. Living inside of this question has been made joyous and companionable because of these friends, mentors, and colleagues.

In my questioning, I have learned from many masterful thinkers and practitioners. I've had the pleasure and honor of working alongside brilliant and visionary people like Fernando Flores, Bob Dunham, and Curt Carlson. Philosophers like John Searle, Bert Dreyfus, and Francisco Varela have deepened my appreciation of the nature of human understanding. Scientists like Carlo Rovelli, Safi Bahcall, and

Terry Winograd have expanded my understanding of the practice of innovation. Embodied practitioners like George Leonard have grounded my explorations into mastery and practice. Future thinkers like Margaret Wheatley and John Gerzema, and the vastly underappreciated genius of the nineteenth-century philosopher, social worker, and management theorist Mary Parker Follett, have informed my thinking and inquiry as to the nature of the generative practices that gender balance brings to innovation.

I could not have done this without the collaboration of two of my siblings David and Penelope Kenny, and for my fabulous writing partner and guide, my daughter Julia Reichard. It's a very long game to write a book by giving birth to an author, but it worked for me.

I am extremely grateful to my wonderful clients who have inspired me with their passion for innovation and their unrelenting inquiry into the science that will make life better for millions of their fellow humans. I wrote this book for them.

Lastly, this book would still be a jumble of drafts without the guiding hand of James Harbeck and the rest of the dedicated individuals at Page Two. It takes a village to publish a book, and I am glad this is the village I found and very grateful for the welcome they have given me.

Notes

Chapter 1: Two Eyes, Two Ears, One Mouth

To quote Klaus Mainzer... Klaus Mainzer, "Interdisciplinarity and innovation dynamics. On convergence of research, technology, economy, and society," *Poiesis & Praxis* 7, no. 4 (June 2011): 275–289, doi.org/10.1007/s10202-011-0088-8.

As Peter Denning and Robert Dunham point out... Peter Denning, "Winning at Innovation," *Computer* 51, no. 10 (October 2018): 32–39, doi.org/10.1109/MC.2018.3971353.

Chapter 2: Innovation Demands Courage

The 2015 Accenture U.S. Innovation Survey... Accenture, "Three Years Later, U.S. Companies Continue to Struggle with Innovation, Accenture Survey Reveals," press release, March 21, 2016, newsroom.accenture.com/news/three-years-later-us-companies-continue-to-struggle-with-innovation-accenture-survey-reveals.htm.

As Douglas Osheroff said... Alexander Bastidas Fry, "Chance Favors the Prepared Mind," Lindau Nobel Laureate Meetings (blog), July 5, 2012, lindau-nobel.org/chance-favors-the-prepared-mind.

it doubles in size in the first year... "Brain Development," First Things First, firstthingsfirst.org/early-childhood-matters/brain-development.

Genius is one percent inspiration... "Edison's Lightbulb," The Franklin Institute, May 19, 2017, fi.edu/history-resources/edisons-lightbulb, (emphasis mine).

popular physicist Carlo Rovelli... Carlo Rovelli, *Helgoland: The Strange and Beautiful Story of Quantum Physics* (New York: Allen Lane, 2021), 93.

This predictive coding... Michael Reilly, "Understanding the Mind," *MIT Technology Review*, August 25, 2021, technologyreview. com/2021/08/25/1032153/mind-editor-letter.

In 2010, Derek Sivers... Derek Sivers, "How to Start a Movement," TED Talk, April 2010, ted.com/talks/ derek_sivers_how_to_start_a_movement.

As Lawrence Fisher writes... Lawrence M. Fisher, "Siri, Who Is Terry Winograd?" *strategy+business* 86, January 3, 2017, strategy-business.com/article/Siri-Who-Is-Terry-Winograd.

Language/Action Perspective... Fernando Flores, "Management and Communication in the Office of the Future," PhD diss., University of California at Berkeley, 1982.

Chapter 3: Power and Commitments

Fernando Flores introduced me... The Listening for Concerns ladder builds on the work of Fernando Flores. See "Recurrent Domains of Human Concern," *Conversations for Action and Collected Essays* (self-pub., 2013), conversationsforaction.com/chapters/ chapter-11-recurrent-domains-human-concerns.

An additional pre-read suggestion... Paul J. Zak, "The Neuroscience of Trust," *Harvard Business Review*, January–February 2017, hbr.org/2017/01/the-neuroscience-of-trust.

Chapter 4: The New View of Projects

the notion of management of work... Steve Andriole, "3 Main Reasons Why Big Technology Projects Fail—& Why Many Companies Should Just Never Do Them," *Forbes*, March 25, 2021, forbes. com/sites/steveandriole/2021/03/25/3-main-reasons-why-big-technology-projects-fail---why-many-companies-should-just-never-do-them.

In a study of some 250 large software projects... Capers Jones, "Software Project Management Practices: Failure Versus Success," *CrossTalk: The Journal of Defense Software Engineering*, October 2004.

In the 1870s, Henri Fayol... Daniel A. Wren, Arthur G. Bedeian, and John D. Breeze, "The Foundations of Henri Fayol's Administrative Theory," *Management Decision* 40, no. 9 (2002): 906–918, faculty.lsu.edu/bedeian/files/the-foundations-of-henri-fayols-administrative-theory.pdf.

human error is the main cause... Micke Ahola, "The Role of Human Error in Successful Cyber Security Breaches," usecure (blog), February 1, 2021, blog.usecure.io/the-role-of-human-error-in-successful-cyber-security-breaches; Capers Jones, "Software Cost Estimating Methods for Large Projects," *CrossTalk* (May 2005).

the experience of repair... Kyle Benson, "Repair Is the Secret Weapon of Emotionally Connected Couples," The Gottman Institute (blog), February 23, 2017, gottman.com/blog/repair-secret-weapon-emotionally-connected-couples.

less "than 3 percent..." Joan Schneider and Julie Hall, "Why Most Product Launches Fail," *Harvard Business Review*, April 2011, hbr.org/2011/04/why-most-product-launches-fail.

the YouTube video... London Business School, "Promise Based Management: Execution Part 1," YouTube video, June 11, 2008, youtube.com/watch?v=tNbU2rQuz_I.

Chapter 5: Empathy and Mastery

joy on the job... Paul J. Zak, "The Neuroscience of Trust," *Harvard Business Review*, January–February 2017, hbr.org/2017/01/the-neuroscience-of-trust.

empathy in action, which is defined... Lin Grensing-Pophal, "What Is Radical Empathy?" *HR Daily Advisor*, December 9, 2021, hrdailyadvisor.blr.com/2021/12/09/what-is-radical-empathy.

empathic design... Dorothy Leonard and Jeffrey F. Rayport, "Spark Innovation Through Empathic Design," *Harvard Business Review*, November–December 1997, hbr.org/1997/11/spark-innovation-through-empathic-design.

TRI researchers... "Sensing Is Believing: More Capable Robot Hands with the Soft Bubble Gripper," Toyota Research Institute, December 9, 2020, tri.global/news/sensing-is-believing-more-sensitive-robot-hands-t-2020-9-9.

As Terry Winograd wrote... Terry Winograd, "Designing a New Foundation for Design," *Communications of the ACM* 49, no. 5 (May 2006): 71, doi.org/10.1145/1125944.1125978.

Hubert Dreyfus defined... Stuart E. Dreyfus, "The Five-Stage Model of Adult Skill Acquisition," *Bulletin of Science, Technology & Society* 24, no. 3 (June 1, 2004): 177–181, doi.org/10.1177/0270467604264992.

E.O. Wilson argued... E. O. Wilson, *Consilience: The Unity of Knowledge* (New York: Vintage, 1999).

Chapter 6: Creating Knowledge

"The hardest thing..." Ben Horowitz, "What's the Most Difficult CEO Skill? Managing Your Own Psychology," Andreessen Horowitz (blog), March 31, 2011, a16z.com/2011/03/31/whats-the-most-difficult-ceo-skill-managing-your-own-psychology. Horowitz is the cofounder and general partner at Andreessen Horowitz.

Professors Nonaka and Takeuchi... Ikujiro Nonaka and Hirotaka Takeuchi, *The Knowledge-Creating Company* (Oxford: Oxford University Press, 1995).

Thinking about our brains as computers... Anya Kamenetz, "The Four Things People Can Still Do Better Than Computers," *Fast Company*, July 19, 2013, fastcompany.com/3014448/ the-four-things-people-can-still-do-better-than-computers.

"Boards with at least..." EY Americas, "Could Gender Equality Be the Innovation Boost Utilities Need?" March 8, 2019, ey.com/en_us/women-power-utilities/ could-gender-equality-be-the-innovation-boost-utilities-need.

The Center for Talent Innovation... EY Americas, "Could Gender Equality Be the Innovation Boost Utilities Need?" March 8, 2019, ey.com/en_us/women-power-utilities/could-gender-equality-be-the-innovation-boost-utilities-need; Erik Larson, "Infographic: Diversity + Inclusion = Better Decision Making at Work," Cloverpop (blog), September 19, 2017, cloverpop.com/blog/ infographic-diversity-inclusion-better-decision-making-at-work.

Gender Diversity Is a Powerful Corporate Performance Lever [table]... EY Americas, "Could Gender Equality Be the Innovation Boost Utilities Need?" March 8, 2019, ey.com/en_us/women-power-utilities/ could-gender-equality-be-the-innovation-boost-utilities-need; Linda-Eling Lee, Ric Marshall, Damion Rallis, and Matt Moscardi, "Women on Boards: Global Trends in Gender Diversity on Corporate Boards," MSCI, November 2015, msci.com/ documents/10199/04b6f646-d638-4878-9c61-4eb91748a82b;

"Women in the Workplace 2021," McKinsey & Company, September 27, 2021, mckinsey.com/featured-insights/diversity-and-inclusion/ women-in-the-workplace; Sue Duris, "What Diversity and Inclusion Mean for Employee Engagement," ICMI, October 1, 2018, icmi.com/resources/2018/what-diversity-and-inclusion-mean-for-employee-engagement; "Credit Suisse Gender 3000 Report Shows Women Hold Almost a Quarter of Board Room Positions Globally," Credit Suisse, press release, September 28, 2021, credit-suisse.com/ about-us-news/en/articles/media-releases/credit-suisse-gender-3000-report-shows-women-hold-almost-a-quart-202109.html.

Conclusion: Three Levels of Innovation Capacity

About three-quarters of venture-capital-backed firms... John McDermott, "Report: 75% of Venture-Backed Start-ups Fail," *Inc.*, September 20, 2012, inc.com/john-mcdermott/report-3-out-of-4-venture-backed-start-ups-fail.html.

Bibliography

Ahola, Micke. "The Role of Human Error in Successful Cyber Security Breaches." usecure (blog). February 1, 2021. blog.usecure.io/the-role-of-human-error-in-successful-cyber-security-breaches.

Austin, J. L. *How to Do Things with Words.* Cambridge, MA: Harvard University Press, 1962.

Bahcall, Safi. *Loonshots: Nurture the Crazy Ideas That Win Wars, Cure Diseases, and Transform Industries.* New York: St. Martin's Griffin, 2019.

Belenky, Mary Field. *Women's Ways of Knowing: The Development of Self, Voice, and Mind.* New York: Basic Books, 1998.

Crawford, Merle, and Anthony Di Benedetto. *New Products Management*, 11th ed. New York: McGraw Hill Education, 2015.

Credit Suisse. "Credit Suisse Gender 3000 Report Shows Women Hold Almost a Quarter of Board Room Positions Globally." Press release. September 28, 2021. credit-suisse.com/about-us-news/en/articles/media-releases/credit-suisse-gender-3000-report-shows-women-hold-almost-a-quart-202109.html.

Dennett, Daniel C. *Consciousness Explained.* New York: Little, Brown and Co., 1991.

Dignan, Aaron. *Brave New Work: Are You Ready to Reinvent Your Organization?* New York: Penguin, 2019.

Dreyfus, Hubert L. *Skillful Coping: Essays on the Phenomenology of Everyday Perception and Action*. Oxford: Oxford University Press, 2014.

Dreyfus, Hubert L. *What Computers Still Can't Do: A Critique of Artificial Reason*. Cambridge, MA: MIT Press, 1992.

Dua, Sameer. *Declaring Breakdowns: Powerfully Creating a Future That Matters, Through 6 Simple Steps*. New Delhi, India: SAGE Publications, 2016.

Duris, Sue. "What Diversity and Inclusion Mean for Employee Engagement." ICMI. October 1, 2018. icmi.com/resources/2018/what-diversity-and-inclusion-mean-for-employee-engagement.

EY Americas. "Could Gender Equality Be the Innovation Boost Utilities Need?" March 8, 2019. ey.com/en_us/women-power-utilities/could-gender-equality-be-the-innovation-boost-utilities-need.

Fayol, Henri. "Henri Fayol Addressed His Colleagues in the Mineral Industry 23 June 1900." In *Industrial and General Administration*, pp. 79–81. Translated by J. A. Coubrough. London, UK: Sir I. Pitman & Sons, 1930. Republished in Daniel A. Wren, Arthur G. Bedeian, and John D. Breeze. "The Foundations of Henri Fayol's Administrative Theory." *Management Decision* 40, no. 9 (2002): 906–918. faculty.lsu.edu/bedeian/files/the-foundations-of-henri-fayols-administrative-theory.pdf.

Feldman Barrett, Lisa. "This Is How Your Brain Makes Your Mind." *MIT Technology Review*. September 28, 2021. technologyreview.com/2021/08/25/1031432/what-is-mind-brain-body-connection.

Ferry, Diane L. Review: *Dynamic Administration: The Collected Papers of Mary Parker Follett*. *Academy of Management Review* 11, no. 2 (1986): 451–454. doi.org/10.2307/258474.

Fisher, Lawrence M. "Siri, Who Is Terry Winograd?" *strategy+business* 86. January 3, 2017. strategy-business.com/article/Siri-Who-Is-Terry-Winograd.

Flores, Fernando. *Conversations for Action and Collected Essays: Instilling a Culture of Commitment in Working Relationships*. Self-pub., 2013.

Follett, Mary Parker. *Creative Experience*. New York: Longmans, Green and Co., 1924.

Follett, Mary Parker. *The New State: Group Organization the Solution of Popular Government*. New York: Longmans, Green and Co., 1918.

Franklin Institute, The. "Edison's Lightbulb." May 19, 2017. fi.edu/history-resources/edisons-lightbulb.

Gerzema, John, and Michael D'Antonio. *The Athena Doctrine: How Women (and the Men Who Think Like Them) Will Rule the Future*. San Francisco: Jossey-Bass, 2013.

Gladwell, Malcolm. *Blink: The Power of Thinking without Thinking*. New York: Little, Brown and Co., 2005.

Grensing-Pophal, Lin. "What Is Radical Empathy?" *HR Daily Advisor*. December 7, 2021. hrdailyadvisor.blr.com/2021/12/09/what-is-radical-empathy.

Leonard, Dorothy, and Jeffrey F. Rayport. "Spark Innovation Through Empathic Design." *Harvard Business Review*. November–December 1997. hbr.org/1997/11/spark-innovation-through-empathic-design.

Leonard, George. *Mastery: The Keys to Success and Long-Term Fulfillment*. New York: Plume, 1992.

Macomber, Harold, and Gregory Howell. "Linguistic Action: Contributing to the Theory of Lean Construction." Proceedings of the 11th Annual Meeting of the International Group for Lean Construction. Blacksburg, Virginia. January 2003. researchgate.net/publication/228918270_Linguistic_Action_Contributing_to_the_Theory_of_Lean_Construction.

Maturana, Humberto R., and Francisco J. Varela. *Autopoiesis and Cognition: The Realization of the Living*. Boston: D. Reidel Publishing Company, 1980.

Maturana, Humberto R., and Francisco J. Varela. *The Tree of Knowledge: The Biological Roots of Human Understanding*. Boston: Shambhala, 1992.

McKinsey & Company. "Women in the Workplace 2021." September 27, 2021. mckinsey.com/featured-insights/diversity-and-inclusion/women-in-the-workplace.

Metcalf, Henry C., and L. Urwick. *Dynamic Administration: The Collected Papers of Mary Parker Follett*. London: Routledge, 2003. doi.org/10.4324/9780203486214.

Nonaka, Ikujiro, and Hirotaka Takeuchi. *The Knowledge-Creating Company: How Japanese Companies Create the Dynamics of Innovation*. Oxford: Oxford University Press, 1995.

Pink, Daniel H. *A Whole New Mind: Why Right-Brainers Will Rule the Future*. New York: Riverhead Books, 2005.

Reilly, Michael. "Understanding the Mind." *MIT Technology Review*. August 25, 2021. technologyreview.com/2021/08/25/1032153/mind-editor-letter.

Rovelli, Carlo. *Reality Is Not What It Seems: The Journey to Quantum Gravity.* Translated by Simon Carnell and Erica Segre. New York: Riverhead Books, 2017.

Searle, John R. *Speech Acts: An Essay in the Philosophy of Language.* Cambridge, UK: Cambridge University Press, 1969.

Senge, Peter M. *The Fifth Discipline: The Art and Practice of the Learning Organization.* New York: Doubleday/Currency, 1990.

Sull, Donald, and Kathleen M. Eisenhardt. *Simple Rules: How to Thrive in a Complex World.* Boston: Mariner Books, 2016.

Torbert, Bill, Susanne Cook-Greuter, Dalmar Fisher, Erica Foldy, Alain Gauthier, Jackie Keeley, David Rooke, Sara Ross, Catherine Royce, Jenny Rudolph, Steve Taylor, and Mariana Tran. *Action Inquiry: The Secret of Timely and Transforming Leadership.* San Francisco: Berrett-Koehler Publishers, 2004.

Wheatley, Margaret J., and Myron Kellner-Rogers. *A Simpler Way.* San Francisco: Berrett-Koehler, 1998.

Wilczek, Frank. *A Beautiful Question: Finding Nature's Deep Design.* New York: Penguin Books, 2015.

Winograd, Terry, and Fernando Flores. *Understanding Computers and Cognition: A New Foundation for Design.* Norwood, NJ: Ablex Publishing, 1986.

About the Author

JENNIFER KENNY is a master of innovation practices. Her work increases the capacity of leaders, teams, and organizations to fuel innovation, performance, and revenue in complex technical environments. She is a speaker and writer who delivers transformational programs globally. Her work is founded on systems thinking and language/action design.

Jennifer has recently been instrumental in preparing the autonomous driving and robotics innovation teams at Toyota Research Institute, the research arm of one of the top fifty smartest companies in the world. Jennifer was CIO at Stanford Research Institute International, where she led the transformation of the information technology organization to drive business innovation. She has worked with Cisco/WebEx, UCSF, Stanford, Wells Fargo, and Accenture. She is also on the faculty of the Thought Leaders Business School, Sydney, Australia.

Her body of work is based on systems thinking—popularized by Peter Senge's book *The Fifth Discipline* and

by Terry Winograd and Fernando Flores (in the paradigm-shifting book *Understanding Computers and Cognition*) as well as Promise-Based Management, popularized by Donald Sull, Charles Spinosa, and others, and the book *Simple Rules: How to Thrive in a Complex World* (coauthored by Donald Sull and Kathleen Eisenhardt). Over the course of twenty-five years, Jennifer has built on and progressed this thinking.

Jennifer is passionate about helping amazing people deliver successful transformation projects by amplifying others. Her goal is to help people who want to become transformational leaders set themselves up to accomplish something they never thought they could.

Jennifer is a certified yoga teacher, mother, avid kayaker, gardener, and Bay Area resident originally from Dublin, Ireland.

Engage with Our Innovation Community

THANK YOU FOR READING *THE INNOVATION MINDSET*.
I hope you found it useful, and I would like to invite
you to join one of our Innovation communities.
Sign up by scanning the unique QR code below and
answering a few questions about yourself.

I mention several engagements with clients, all of
whom I've worked with through my company,
100% Capacity. We deliver progress with leadership
programs that bring the Innovation Mindset to life,
creating practices that drive sustained success and
deliver improved results.

If you would like to learn more about these programs
or book an in-person conference speech to bring
the Innovation Mindset to your enterprise, please visit
our website at 100capacity.com or get in touch via
email at info@100capacity.com. You can also order
bulk copies of this book at a discounted rate.

Made in the USA
Las Vegas, NV
07 February 2023

67064952R00121